SERIOUS
FUN
in English
BOOK 1

Kathryn Fitzgerald and Tania Roxborogh

NELSON
A Cengage Company

Serious Fun in English Book 1
1st Edition
Kathryn Fitzgerald
Tania Roxborogh

Cover design: Cheryl Smith, Macarn Design
Text designer: Cheryl Smith, Macarn Design
Production controller: Siew Han Ong

Any URLs contained in this publication were checked for currency during the production process. Note, however, that the publisher cannot vouch for the ongoing currency of URLs.

Acknowledgements
The authors and publisher wish to thank the following people and organisations for permission to use the resources in this textbook.

Pages 23 and 28, *We, Who Live in Darkness* by Hone Tuwhare, courtesy of the Estate of Hone Tuwhare; page 32, *Kuramārōtini*, courtesy of Briar Wood; page 34, Kupe, and the discovery of Aotearoa (New Zealand) courtesy of Robbie Whitmore; page 36, *Waka 86*, courtesy of Robert Sullivan and AUP; page 43, *The Korean Cinderella* by Shirley Climo, 1993, courtesy of Harper Collins UK; page 61, Words can Kill, courtesy of Eva Der; page 64, Silent Killers courtesy of Christine von Arnim.

For product information and technology assistance,
in Australia call **1300 790 853**;
in New Zealand call **0800 449 725**

For permission to use material from this text or product, please email **aust.permissions@cengage.com**

National Library of New Zealand Cataloguing-in-Publication Data
A catalogue record for this book is available from the National Library of New Zealand

978 0 17 044882 6

Cengage Learning Australia
Level 7, 80 Dorcas Street
South Melbourne, Victoria Australia 3205

Cengage Learning New Zealand
Unit 4B Rosedale Office Park
331 Rosedale Road, Albany, North Shore 0632, NZ

For learning solutions, visit **cengage.co.nz**

Printed in China by 1010 Printing International Limited
2 3 4 5 6 7 29 28 27 26 25

Note to teachers and students:

Serious Fun in English is primarily written as a supplementary English workbook filled with short, student-centred activities which focus on learning core skills and using a variety of vocabulary, language and punctuation activities that draw upon comprehension skills.

Each of the sections focuses on an area of English study (such as close reading or making connections) and has a wide range of activities: puzzles, spelling activities, word finds, punctuation activities, crosswords and dictionary skills as well as opportunities for original art and original stories via scaffolding. The level of difficulty of the tasks in each section range from very simple/straightforward all the way through to challenging/extension. A lot of the vocabulary used in the tasks comes from the first 1000 words of the Academic Word List.

Students can work through the book on their own, via set class work but the book can also be used as in-class study. There is opportunity for teachers to extend on the tasks included with scope for pair and group work to enhance the learning and enjoyment.

The five sections are each based around an overarching theme and the vocabulary used in the activities has been selected to complement that theme.

Contents

Ko wai au? Who am I?

The purpose of this section is to help you think about who you are, learn some new words, do some creative writing, practise your spelling and have some fun.

PART ONE

All about me

A **My name**

Write down your full name and find out the origin and meaning of each name. For example, first name 'Tania', origin Russian, means 'The Fairy Queen'.

First name: _____

Origin and Meaning: _____

_____

Second name: _____

Origin and Meaning: _____

_____

Third name: _____

Origin and Meaning: _____

_____

Surname (family name): _____

Origin and Meaning: _____

_____

Your nickname: _____

Explain how you got your nickname: _____

_____

B **My place in this world**

Another way people can get to know you is to find out a little about where you live and/or where you and/or your family come from. Write either your pepeha or a short descriptor that describes your connections to place.

1 The place where your ancestors are from.

_____

2 The name of your iwi/ethnicity.

_____

 ISBN: 9780170448826

3 Your mountain or the mountain closest to where you live.

_____

4 Your river/sea or the water close to where you live.

_____

5 The name of the region you live in.

_____

6 The name of your school.

_____

7 Your name.

_____

C My picture

Draw a sketch or cartoon of yourself or how you would like to be identified.

D My family crest

Marae and many families have a visual representation of their family history in the form of a crest or carving. Usually there is an animal such as a bird, and/or a landmark as well as a short saying or motto, which identifies the wider family group.

Create your own personal crest, shield or design that represents who you are and where you are from. Write your motto. We have given you some examples here for inspiration but you may also like to use the internet to search for examples of other family crests.

Your family/whānau saying or motto: _____

_____

  ISBN: 9780170448826

My space

Use the template below to create your dream bedroom. Choose the colours and objects that you think will tell others about your personality, interests and hobbies.

My bedroom

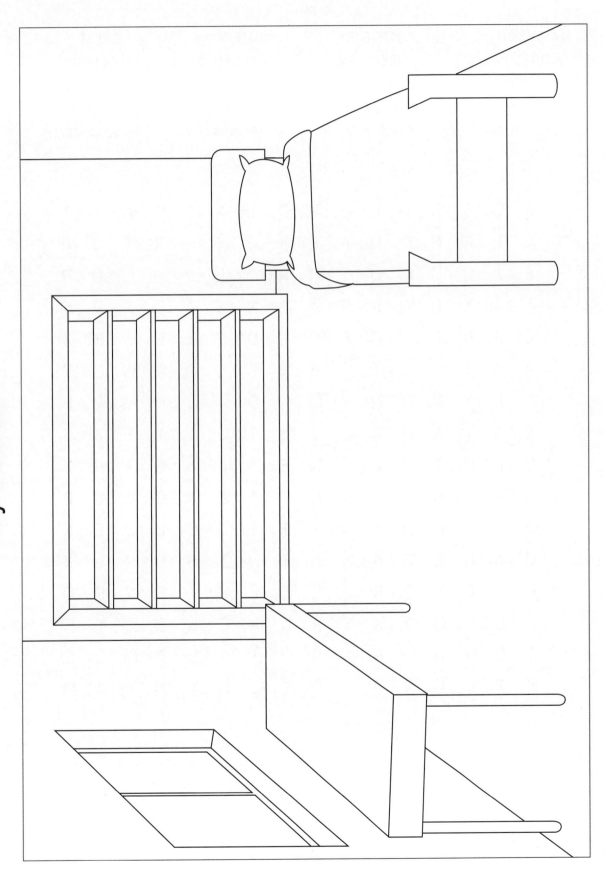

Word search

Find the words listed below and circle them in the puzzle. Words can be found going forwards, backwards and diagonal. Good luck!

AMBITION	ANCESTORS	AOTEAROA	CREST
ETHNICITY	FOREBEARS	GENEALOGY	IDENTITY
INHERITED	ITINERANT	LANDMARK	PARENTAGE
PEPEHA	PRECURSOR	PROVERB	SETTLED
SYMBOLISM	TRAIT	WHAKAPAPA	WHAKATAUKĪ

```
R O S R U C E R P L A T R A I T
G L A N D M A R K O Y Z X T J R
E T Q D M Q G N R T L J N N D R
N A Y K W R R A I N X A Q S V M
E P B T L B E C L D R X R W D T
A A I J D T I B R E E O M W G Y
L P X N O N V M N D T L H M V P
O A Y A H K L I S S G A T E Z S
G K N T X E T N E I K W G T R X
Y A E B I I R C O A L A B A E P
B H Z R D T N I T I T O E Q E S
Q W N E C A N A T N T B B P L K
M G B V Q R U E E E E I E M R Q
L D B O G K E R D R D H B X Y N
T D M R Ī B A S O I A B T M L S
K Z L P R P J F T Q N Y W X A M
```

 ISBN: 9780170448826

Using the best word, spelling words correctly, understanding the meaning of words — these are essential skills to better communication. The following exercises use words linked to the topic of identity as well as some words you should know to help you in your reading at high school.

PART TWO

Words! Words! Words!

A Match the definitions

Match the definitions on the right with the words listed on the left. The first one has been done for you.

a environment
b individual
c evidence
d landmark
e benefit
f identified
g involved
h ambition
i available
j area
k traits

1 proved or recognised something as being certain
2 something that is good or an advantage
3 an area or surroundings, especially where people live or work
4 included; complicated, detailed
5 a region, district; a section, portion, part
6 a single thing, being, instance or item
7 suitable or ready for use
8 something that proves or disproves something else
9 a strong desire for success, achievement or distinction
10 distinguishing characteristics or qualities, especially of one's personal nature
11 a clearly seen object or formation that serves as a guide especially for travellers

B Complete the sentence

Put the words from the list above (in Task **A**) correctly into the gaps to complete each sentence.

1 The animals at the zoo prefer this _____ because it is like their natural habitat.

2 A gold medal can be won by one _____.

3 The police gather _____ at a crime scene.

4 I have many of my father's _____ — all the silly ones.

5 There is no _____ in studying only the night before an exam, so I might as well finish my game.

6 The thieves were arrested because they were _____ by the witness.

7 Aunty always tells us not to get _____ in the school squabbles, but we can't help it.

8 My _____ is to be a pilot, but my granddad hopes I'll take over his butcher shop.

9 One Tree Hill is an Auckland _____ that is currently named 'No Tree Hill' by some locals.

10 The _____ _____ outside of town is where the council will build the new skate park.

C Spelling

For each sentence below, there are two words misspelled. Circle the errors and then rewrite the words correctly.

1 We welcome everyone, regardless of their ethicnity or rilegion.

_____   _____

2 The dictionery did not have any defenition that I understood. I'll ask Google instead.

_____   _____

3 I find the caracthers in this novel really annoiying.

_____   _____

4 Mr T's interpratition of the Rangi and Papatūānuku myth was hilerious.

_____   _____

5 Our classroom is not availeable during lunchtimes because our teacher dose not want it made messy.

_____   _____

D Synonyms

Circle the synonyms that match with the word in the left column.

WORD	SYNONYMS
whakapapa	genealogy pattern parentage library cushion forebears fireplace bloodline adjective ancestor
symbolism	cross metaphor fish blanket cat imagery scooter bucket representation
ethnicity	adventure transport origin identity nationality canvas race country
inherited	friend computer acquired television transmitted classroom bequeathed
specific	mirror bus definite agonies principal exact smile precise
crest	feathers shops magazine badge army motorway insignia book shield
itinerant	gypsy carpet nomadic camping dishwasher vagabond market wandering
significant	ancestor important trivial detention serious homework vital
similar	pedigree feature identical climate like bathroom occupation kindred relatives honey same
proverb	library adage Bible saying homework moral Lego printer truism

    ISBN: 9780170448826

E Description of a place

1 Using some of the words from the table on the previous page (in Task **D**), write a short descriptive piece which describes to the reader a place that is special to you.

_____

_____

_____

_____

_____

_____

_____

_____

_____

2 Underline or highlight the words you have used from the word bank.
3 Write down your favourite line here.

_____

F Punctuation practice: capital letters

Remember, we use a capital letter at the start of a sentence and for proper nouns (like people's names or names of cities). Rewrite the follow sentences, putting the capital letters in the correct place.

a my uncle is called john.

_____

b he's dad's little brother.

_____

c he doesn't like me calling him 'uncle john'.

_____

d instead, i'm to call him 'better brother'.

_____

e dad says to call him 'pain in the butt brother'.

_____

f i think i'll stick with uncle john.

_____

g i don't want to get between dad and his brother.

_____

Identity crossword

Below is a crossword of words connected to identity you should be familiar with.

ACROSS
1   Your extended family.
2   The unique set of behaviours, beliefs, attitudes a person exhibits.
3   Your family tree; your ancestors; genealogy.
7   Your family tree; your ancestors; whakapapa.
8   To gain or receive an object or a characteristic from another.
9   A distinguishing characteristic or quality, especially of one's personal nature.
11 A short, wise saying, which shows some recognisable truth about people, society, etc.; whakataukī.
12 A social group that shares a common and distinctive culture, religion, language, etc.
13 A distinguishing landscape feature marking a site or location.

DOWN
1   A short, wise saying, which shows some recognisable truth about people, society etc.; proverb.
4   An earnest desire for a thing or goal .
5   Who a person is: the qualities, beliefs, etc. that distinguish or identify a person.
6   Something used to represent something else.
10 An ornament or badge worn to identify a family or regiment, for example.
11 A formal personal introduction, which follows a set sequence.

Let's read and write

A Match the terms

Complete the table below by selecting the correct language term from the list below to match with the definition and example.

listing	metaphor	alliteration
adjective	personal pronoun	verb
imperative	short sentence	adverb

TERM	DEFINITION	EXAMPLE
a	Describing word; describes the noun.	hot, cold, blue, big, small
b	Describing word; describes the verb (how or when or where the action is done).	He smiled **sadly**. They were **nowhere**. **Yesterday**, I went to the park.
c	The repetition of consonant sounds.	**T**iny **T**im **t**rod on **D**on's **t**oes (the 'd' is also an example)
d	A doing word.	I **ate** my lunch, then **walked** to class.
e	Ordering or commanding an action.	Don't hit your sister.
f	Related words or phrases arranged as a list.	I eat toast, cereal and a banana for breakfast.
g	One- to three-word sentences, often phrases.	Try it. Now.
h	A comparison between two things where one thing is said to be another.	The playground **is a jungle** and all the students **are wild animals**.
i	A word that stands in place of a proper noun.	he, she, me, you, I, we, us, them, they

ISBN: 9780170448826

B Identity poem

Read this poem and complete the tasks that follow.

The Tania Roxborogh Poem

Tania Roxborogh <u>is an uneven package</u>
<u>of prized mementos and incomplete dreams</u>
stuck together with <u>unreliable</u> tape.

Tania Roxborogh is a blue painted rocking horse
racing always into the dawn.
She is <u>soft</u> tussock grass
dancing in the breeze.

<u>Whenever I</u> glance in mirrors,
child Tania stares out, <u>wide eyes warning</u>
that I must keep my promises.
Tania Roxborogh is a <u>second-hand</u> car and
a piece of heaven.

Tania Roxborogh is not her real name.
Her true identity <u>lost</u> by careless hands.

<u>Watch out!</u> <u>She bites!</u>
Scattered hopes and hard won gains
are sharp edged.
If you feel <u>a sting, a cut, a bruising</u>
in your soul,
it just might be

by Tania Roxborogh

a _____

b _____

c _____

d _____

e _____

f _____

g _____

h _____

i _____

j _____

1 In the boxes provided, label the language features and parts of speech from the list below. Refer to the chart on page 13 for help.

adjective	metaphor	adjective	adjective	imperative
listing	adverb	verb	alliteration	short sentence

ISBN: 9780170448826

2 Write your own identity poem. Use the questions below to help you shape your poem.

a What type of package are you? Size, shape, colour, texture.

_____

b How are you held together?

_____

c How might you be delivered (and received)?

_____

d What kind of toy are you?

_____

e How might you be used?

_____

f What part of the whenua/landscape are you? What might someone else do on you?

_____

g When you look in the mirror, what do you see looking back?

_____

h What kind of transport are you?

_____

i Where might you go?

_____

j What kind of extraterrestrial (not from Earth) might you be?

_____

k Where does your name come from? How many letters of the alphabet is it?

_____

l What command or warning might you speak?

_____

m You are part of many pieces. What could that be (e.g. marbles, puzzles, Lego, jellybeans, M&Ms, etc.)?

_____

n Where might you and the other pieces be found?

_____

3 Write your identity poem in the spaces provided.

_____

_____ is a

a _____

b _____

c _____

_____ is a

d _____

e _____

_____ .

f _____

Whenever I _____ in mirrors,

g _____

_____

_____ is a

h _____

i _____

j and _____

_____ is

k _____

l _____

m _____

n _____ .

by _____

ISBN: 9780170448826

C Match the terms

Complete the table below by selecting the correct language term from the list below to match with the definition and example.

repetition proper nouns rhyme

pun rhetorical question onomatopoeia

hyperbole personification simile

TERM	DEFINITION	EXAMPLE
a	When a non-living thing is given living characteristics or when a non-human thing is given human characteristics.	The lift groaned on the way down.
b	Nouns that refer to a specific person, place, object or period of time.	Mr Jones; Hamilton; National Heart Foundation
c	An expression that plays on different meanings of the same word or phrase.	I've been to the dentist so many times, I know the drill.
d	Words or statements used more than once for effect.	The room was cold. Too cold to think.
e	A word in which its sound imitates or suggests the meaning or noise of the action described.	crash, gurgle
f	A question in which an answer is not expected (asked to involve the audience).	Have you ever thought about donating to charity?
g	The repetition of words with similar sounds.	There was an old horse from Cant**ucket**, who ate from a rusted brown b**ucket**.
h	A phrase that compares two things, using 'like' or 'as' and sometimes 'than'.	They behave **like** monkeys in the classroom, but are **as well behaved as** royalty in the playground.
i	An exaggeration.	I'm so tired, I could sleep for a month.

D Using texts as inspiration

Read the piece below and complete the exercises that follow.

First Encounter

Let me tell you about my encounter with Mr Roger, the black and white tom cat we used to have: <u>fat-faced, sleepy</u>-looking half-closed eyes and <u>the deadliest claws in Northland</u>. One afternoon I found him napping in the sun in the hay barn, right up the top near the skylight. I'd climbed up for a rest and thought, because Mr Roger looked so content, I'd give him a bit of a pat. Despite the warnings from Dad not to trust him, I stroked his head and then gave him a few long gentle strokes down his back. Mr Roger purred, shifted and stood to 'receive' my attentions. He smiled as cats do, the <u>sound of his purrs</u> filling the cavity <u>between me, my eaten lunch, the bales and the roof of the barn.</u> Mr Roger stepped on to my lap, his tail high and that was my error — <u>thinking he was safe, thinking I was safe.</u> I leant forward to allow him to smooch me when suddenly he's swiped my face with a one-two strike, one of his front claws catching on the skin of my cheek, another hooking into the bridge of my nose. <u>The pain was like a knife cut.</u> I yelped and fell back but he wasn't finished with me (maybe because he was still attached to my face). He was <u>hissing and spitting with an intense</u> rage I'd never imagined coming from a cat!

I don't know how I got free from him but before I could kick him away, he leapt off the bales and darted out of the barn. <u>My face was a horror movie.</u> Large drops of blood fell on my t-shirt and arm. By the time I was outside, I was already crying tears of pain and anger. Mum told me later that when I walked into the house she thought I'd had a fight with the lawnmower <u>and the lawnmower had won,</u> there was so much blood.

I hated that cat and I've still got the scar on my nose to remind me.

by T.K. Roxborogh ©

a _____

b _____

c _____

d _____

e _____

f _____

g _____

h _____

i _____

1 In the spaces on page 18, label the underlined phrases with the correct language feature from the list below. Refer to the charts on pages 13 and 17 for help.

metaphor   simile   personification   hyperbole/exaggeration

alliteration   repetition   use of adjectives   onomatopoeia   listing

2 Your turn: write about the first encounter you had with someone or something. Use the sentence prompts to help you plan your short piece.

a Choose a person or animal you met for the first time.

_____

b Write two colour words to describe your someone/something.

_____ and _____

c What were you doing?

_____

_____

d How were you feeling? Why?

_____

_____

e What was the person or thing doing?

_____

_____

f Describe the first thing that happened when you met this person/thing.

_____

_____

_____

g What is one thing your person or thing is the best or worst at?

_____

_____

h What lesson did you learn from your first encounter?

_____

_____

_____

3 Using the spaces below, create a storyboard of a first encounter you had with the person or animal.

Title _____

1

[ ]

_____
_____
_____
_____

2

[ ]

_____
_____
_____
_____

3

[ ]

_____
_____
_____
_____

4

[ ]

_____
_____
_____
_____

5

[ ]

_____
_____
_____
_____

6

[ ]

_____
_____
_____
_____

7

[ ]

_____
_____
_____
_____

8

[ ]

_____
_____
_____
_____

9

[ ]

_____
_____
_____
_____

 ISBN: 9780170448826

4   Now, write your description. We have given you a starter and an ending to help.

Let me tell you about _____

_____

_____

_____

_____

_____

_____

_____

_____

_____

_____

_____

_____

_____

_____

_____

_____

_____

_____

_____

_____

and I've still got the _____ to prove it.

Give your description to a friend or family member to read. Get them to give you a review of your description:

Signed _____   Date _____

E Word table

Use the clues to help you find the words in the table. We have written some letters to help you get started.

1 A social group that shares a common and distinctive culture, religion, language, etc.

2 The study of family ancestries and histories.

3 Someone who comes before, like a father, grandfather.

4 Those people from whom you are descended, like your great-great-grandparents.

5 A person who moves from place to place, is not settled or fixed.

6 Another word for those relatives who have come before us.

7 Ancestral lines; lines of descent; lineage; ancestry. Often used with animals.

8 (Of an object or a characteristic) Gained or received from another.

9 Another word describing qualities that are inherited (see **7** above).

1	E		H		C			Y
2		E		E			O	G
3	P	R	E	C				
4			C	E			O	R
5	I				E		A	N
6		O	R		B	E		
7			D				E	
8			H	E	R			E
9	P		R				G	E

Our beginnings

As a teenager living in New Zealand/Aotearoa, you will hopefully be familiar with the creation story of our country. In this section, we will be looking closely at *how* writers have told stories of our beginning.

Ranginui and Papatūānuku are the first parents: the sky father and the earth mother who lie locked together in a tight embrace. They have many children, all of whom are male, who are forced to live in the cramped darkness between them. Tūmatauenga, the fiercest of the children, proposes that the best solution to their predicament is to kill their parents. But his brother Tāne-mahuta disagrees, suggesting that it is better to push them apart, to let Ranginui be as a stranger to them in the sky above while Papatūānuku will remain below to nurture them.

PART ONE

Let's start at the beginning

 A First impressions

This poem, written by Hone Tuwhare, deals with this creation myth. Read it and complete the tasks that follow.

We, Who Live in Darkness

It has been a long long time of it
wriggling and squirming in the swamp of night.
And what was time, anyway? Black intensities
of black on black on black feeding on itself?
Something immense? Immeasureless?

No more.
There just had to be a beginning somehow.
For on reaching the top of a slow rise suddenly
eyes I never knew I possessed were stung by it
forcing me to hide my face in the earth.

It was light, my brothers. Light.
A most beautiful sight infiltered past
the armpit hairs of the father. Why, I could
even see to count all the fingers of my hands
held out to it; see the stain — the clutch of
good earth on them.

But then he moved.
And darkness came down even more oppressively
it seemed and I drew back tense; angry.

Brothers, let us kill him — push him off.

by Hone Tuwhare

1 Use the space below to record your first impressions of the poem. You can write in bullet points, draw some images or write in full sentences. What words stand out to you? What images do they create in your mind? Sketch these.

2 Whose point of view do you think the poem is from?

I think this poem is told from _____'s point of view because it says

'_____'.

3 Poems are written to sound beautiful, to tell a story or to share a message.

a Which one is this poem?

_____

b I think this because ... *(quote from the poem)*

_____.

 ISBN: 9780170448826

B Tone

All pieces of writing have an overall tone, which falls firstly into the broad category of positive or negative. Basically, if there are more positive than negative words, it is a positive piece.

1   Reread the poem. Do you think this has a positive or negative tone? _____

2   Highlight the words in the list below that are used in the poem to help contribute to the overall _____ tone of the piece.

long time	wriggling	squirming	swamp
night	black	intensifies	feeding
immense	immeasureless	beginning	top
rise	suddenly	eyes	possessed
never knew	stung	forcing	hide
light	beautiful	sight	past
stain	clutch	good earth	oppressively
tense	angry	kill	push

C Describing your experience

Using the space below, take 8–10 of Tuwhare's words and write a short paragraph describing a time that you experienced darkness. For example, when camping, in a glow-worm cave, driving on a country road in winter, …

_____
_____
_____
_____
_____
_____
_____
_____
_____
_____
_____
_____
_____
_____
_____
_____
_____
_____
_____
_____

By choosing these specific words, Tuwhare makes us feel like we are experiencing the darkness alongside the narrator. Tuwhare uses specifically chosen words to create a negative tone, which helps build up a sense of darkness, emptiness and being trapped. We feel excited for the narrator when he sees light for the first time and his anger when it is taken away from him; Tuwhare makes us feel that it is okay for the narrator to kill 'him' and that it is justified.

D Creating your own poem

Select at least five words from the list on page 25. Then just jot down the first things that come to mind — this is called free verse. Don't worry about correct punctuation. (If you look carefully at Tuwhare's poem, you will see that it has sentences that go over multiple lines, as he breaks them up to emphasise certain points. This is called *enjambment*.)

My five words:

1

2

3

4

5

 ISBN: 9780170448826

1 Below is a crossword of language features you should be familiar with. Refer to the glossary if you need help.

ACROSS

6   In poetry; when a sentence is over more than one line.
9   Creation of a particular mood in a text.
10 A question designed to make a point and get the audience thinking.
11 Stand in place of a name and make reader feel involved. (2 words)
12 Consonant sounds repeated in two or more word close together.
13 Building a clear picture in the reader's mind.
14 A deliberate exaggeration, not meant to be taken literally.

DOWN

1   Words used to describe a particular action or state.
2   Direct command to do something.
3   Repeated word or phrases for emphasis.
4   Words that sound like the noise they are describing.
5   Comparing two things to imply a figurative similarity.
7   Comparing two different things with 'like' or 'as'.
8   Giving nonliving things human-like qualities.

2 In Tuwhare's poem, he uses several language features effectively. Correctly label the following language features on the poem. Refer to the glossary if you need help.

repetition   imperative   verbs   imagery

personal pronouns   alliteration   rhetorical question

We, Who Live in Darkness

It has been a <u>long long</u> time of it

<u>wriggling</u> and <u>squirming</u> in the swamp of night.

And <u>what was time, anyway?</u> Black intensities

of black on black on black feeding on itself?

Something <u>immense</u>? <u>Immeasureless</u>?

No more.

There just had to be a beginning somehow.

For on reaching the top of a slow rise suddenly

eyes <u>I</u> never knew <u>I</u> possessed were stung by it

forcing <u>me</u> to hide <u>my</u> face in the earth.

It was light, my brothers. Light.

<u>A most beautiful sight infiltered past</u>

<u>the armpit hairs of the father. Why, I could</u>

<u>even see to count all the fingers of my hands</u>

<u>held out to it; see the stain — the clutch of</u>

<u>good earth on them.</u>

But then he moved.

And darkness came down even more oppressively

it seemed and I drew back tense; angry.

Brothers, <u>let us kill him — push him off</u>.

by Hone Tuwhare

a _____

b _____

c _____

d _____

e _____

f _____

g _____

3 The following language features occur often in poetry.

    a Find them in the word search.

ALLITERATION   ASSONANCE   ENJAMBMENT   IMPERATIVE
METAPHOR   PERSONIFICATION   RHYME   RHYTHM
SIMILE   STANZA   VERB

```
P  D  E  S  T  A  N  Z  A  E  R  G  A  M  O
Y  E  Y  C  O  C  C  F  N  R  O  K  L  P  O
I  O  R  X  N  X  U  J  U  V  H  Q  L  Q  C
S  Q  O  S  V  A  A  L  E  C  P  K  I  R  U
E  B  L  J  O  M  N  R  X  A  A  I  T  H  L
L  A  J  R  B  N  B  O  J  V  T  U  E  Y  T
N  P  C  M  H  I  I  N  S  R  E  Q  R  M  J
O  M  E  X  V  Y  V  F  B  S  M  I  A  E  Q
O  N  O  T  K  Z  T  G  I  I  A  J  T  P  E
T  D  H  Z  U  Q  E  H  F  C  H  D  I  B  S
P  W  B  D  C  L  E  U  M  M  A  V  O  Y  X
Z  F  N  F  I  N  M  D  F  V  T  T  N  H  H
H  Q  U  M  O  Q  G  F  R  J  C  W  I  I  T
E  V  I  T  A  R  E  P  M  I  L  T  E  O  W
Z  S  R  H  F  M  Z  G  A  B  D  D  M  M  N
```

    b Colour red the techniques which enhance what we see.

    c Colour blue the techniques which emphasise sound.

4 As well as identifying the tone and which language features have been used, a trick to understanding a poem is to read only the title and the last line(s) together. This can help you understand what the overall purpose/aim/theme/idea of the poem is.

    a Write down the title and last sentence of the poem.

    _____

    _____

    _____

    b What might this information tell you about Tuwhare's attitude to what the narrator did?

    _____

    _____

    _____

5 Using the box below, fill it full of visual images (objects/toys/places) that you would associate with this poem. You can draw these images, cut them out of a magazine or print them from an internet search.

'We, Who Live in Darkness' — a poetry box

 ISBN: 9780170448826

Making connections

There are three main types of connections that good readers make as they are reading. You probably recognise these from primary school:

- Text to Self
- Text to Text
- Text to World.

Making connections is when you can recognise links, commonalities and relationships across seemingly disconnected texts. These links could come under:

- Knowledge, ideas and experience
- Purposes and audiences (why it is written and who it is written for)
- Language features
- Structure.

 Kupe and Kuramārōtini

As well as knowing the Māori creation myth, hopefully you are aware of the story of how New Zealand/Aotearoa was discovered.

> Kupe is a legendary figure in Māori culture and he was the one, alongside Kuramārōtini, who discovered New Zealand Aotearoa. Kupe set out from Hawaiki to destroy an octopus and the journey led him to find New Zealand/Aotearoa.

In this section, we are going to look at two texts that deal with this myth from Māori culture and draw connections between them. Being able to recognise connections (both similarities and differences) is a key skill in being a good reader.

Kuramārōtini

The first text is a poem by Briar Wood and is told from Kuramārōtini's perspective. But first, we need to make sure we understand all of the words that appear in the poem.

1   Prereading vocabulary work
    Look up the following words in a Māori–English dictionary (try maoridictionary.co.nz) and write the definition beside it (**d** has been done for you).

   a hoa _____

   b ākuanei _____

   c Matahourua _____

   d Hoturapa _The name of Kuramārōtini's husband and the friend Kupe threw overboard._

   e Aotearoa _____

Look up the following words in an English dictionary.

f   navigator_____

g   inveterate _____

h   loomed _____

i   radiant _____

2   Choose two words from the list of Māori words and two more words from the list of English
words, then write several sentences using the words correctly.

_____

_____

_____

_____

_____

_____

_____

3   Read this poem.

Kuramārōtini

So the story goes
that trickster Kupe
cheated his friend
into diving overboard
to free the lines
then paddled rapidly away.

Some hoa.
Best to know that
legendary navigators take huge risks
and do not make the safest companions.

Ākuanei —
she asked herself —
what do I want —
home in Hawaiki
or the travelling years?

What does he want —
the waka my father gifted?
Matahourua and me?

Or maybe unhappiness
with the man she'd married
drove her to the coast.
It's possible —
she was curious and Hoturapa wasn't
the kind of man who liked a journey
so she chose Kupe.

Yet even an inveterate traveller
might become weary in a waka
on the open sea,
looking out for landfall.

Travelling direct to her destination —
as the future loomed towards her
she named that radiant land
on the horizon
Aotearoa.

by Briar Wood

4 Visualisation. Use the space below to sketch something you imagined as you read the poem on page 32.

The second text we are going to look at is a short text about Kupe and how he discovered New Zealand/Aotearoa. Read this short account.

Kupe, and the discovery of Aotearoa (New Zealand)

In Hawaiki lived a canoe maker by the name of Toto. Toto fabricated two huge ocean-going canoes from a large tree. One canoe he named Aotea and the other he named Matahourua. Toto gave his canoe named Aotea to one of his daughters, Rongorongo, and the other canoe named Matahourua to his other daughter, Kura. It happened that Kupe desired Kura very much. However, Kura was already the wife of Kupe's cousin Hoturapa.

When Hoturapa and Kupe were out fishing one day, Kupe ordered Hoturapa to dive down and free Kupe's fishing line, which had become tangled. When Hoturapa dived into the sea to free the tangled line, Kupe sliced through the anchor rope of the canoe, and began to row furiously back to shore. Hoturapa drowned, but his family were suspicious of the circumstances surrounding his death. It was, in fact, a plan on Kupe's part to take Hoturapa's wife Kura.

In order to avoid vengeance from Hoturapa's family, Kupe and his own family left Hawaiki in Kura's canoe Matahourua. After some time of navigating, Kupe's wife Hine Te Aparangi sighted the islands of New Zealand, which appeared as land lying beneath a cloud. Because of this, they named the islands Aotearoa, Land of the Long White Cloud.

As Kupe and his crew were sailing along the coast of this new land, they disturbed a giant octopus, who was hiding in a coastal cave. The octopus whipped its enormous tentacles around the canoe, intent on devouring the whole canoe. During the furious battle which followed with the sea monster, it became obvious that the Matahourua was in great danger of breaking up.

However, Kupe suddenly had an idea, and threw a large water gourd overboard. The octopus, thinking that a man had fallen over, released its tentacles from the Matahourua and turned to attack the gourd. Kupe seized this opportunity, and waited until the octopus was entwined around the gourd. Kupe then attacked the head of the octopus with his adze, and the octopus died.

With his adze, Kupe then cut several islands away from the South Island, and several islands away from the North Island, including the island of Kapiti. He remained for a short while in modern Wellington, before continuing northwards up the coast of the North Island, naming various islands, rivers and harbours on the way. Kupe then returned to Hawaiki, telling everybody of this distant cloud capped and high rising land which he had discovered.

He gave instructions on how to return to this new land, but said that he himself would not be returning.

Abridged from *New Zealand in History*

Compare and contrast concept map. In this section, we will be focusing on connecting Text to Text, looking at the previous story and poem about the discovery of New Zealand/Aotearoa. Fill in the concept map with as much information as you can.

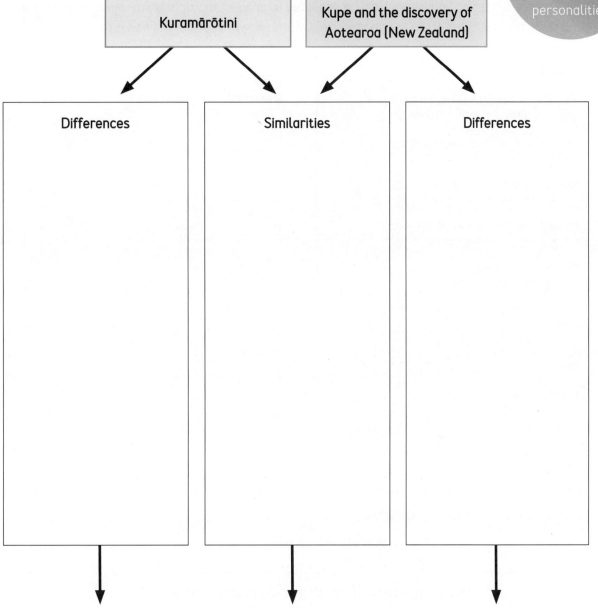

Kuramārōtini

Kupe and the discovery of Aotearoa (New Zealand)

Differences

Similarities

Differences

What did I learn? What is important for me to remember? Why would there be differences between these texts?

Push yourself

A Understanding 'Waka 86'

When you reach senior English, you will be expected to connect multiple texts together. Here is a third text, another poem. Read the poem carefully and answer the questions that follow.

Waka 86

I am Kupe. I have the credit for finding
this new land, the parts of which

I named with parts of me, including
my son — I have left my son here,

the gods were appeased.
My soul will never forget this.

I have been quoted many times,
e hoki a Kupe? Did Kupe return?

The saying is meant to politely
refuse a request. But I do

return to this land. Thoughts
I placed here keep returning

to my ears. I am sorry
for correcting the saying,

but I have been returning
for a very long time now.

by Robert Sullivan

---

1 Use this space to draw or sketch an illustration for the poem.

---

2 a Who is the narrator of the poem? _____

b Who is the narrator speaking to? _____

c What two things did the narrator leave behind? _____

_____

d What is the main message the narrator wishes the reader to understand?

_____

_____

e The word 'return' is repeated many times throughout this poem. When you think of this word, what ideas or other words come to mind for you? List them below.

_____

_____

_____

f For what is the narrator apologising and why is it necessary?

_____

_____

Connecting multiple texts

1 Use the following diagram to help you work through possible connections across these three texts.

We, Who Live in Darkness

Waka 86

Kupe, and the discovery of
Aotearoa (New Zealand)

2 Complete the following sentence starters.

a The character of _____ in '(insert text name) _____'
is like _____ in '(insert text name) _____' because

_____

_____.

b The event of _____ in '(insert text name) _____'
is different to '(insert text name) _____'. I think this is because

_____

_____.

c From these three texts, I have learned _____

_____

_____.

1 Crack the challenging code

What is the name of the person Kupe gave a gift to and what was the gift? Use the clues to crack the code and work out the name of one person and the name of the gift they received from Kupe.

These are the clues to what goes into the spaces above:
— there are two words
— eight of the letters are vowels
— four letters are used twice
— two letters are used only once
— one word has twice as many letters as the other word.

2 Punctuation practice with the comma and the apostrophe

The commas and apostrophes have been removed from the following sentences. Put them back in. (Hint: The structure of the sentences is very similar to that in the story on page 34.)

a When competitive swimmers Conrad and Liam were out swimming one day Liam told Conrad to dive down and free Liams goggles which were stuck under a rock.

b When Conrad dived into the sea to get the goggles Liam swam back to shore and left him there in the cold water breaking the rules of always swimming in pairs.

c Conrad got hypothermia and couldn't race the next day and his family were suspicious of Liams part in what happened.

d In order to avoid trouble from Conrads family Liam and his own family left Tolaga Bay.

e Because Conrad said it wasnt really Liams fault he should return so they could race together again.

3 Push yourself with language features. To succeed in English, you need to have a good understanding of language features. Fill in the chart below with either examples from the three poems in this section or your own examples.

TERM	DEFINITION	EXAMPLE
Alliteration	The repetition of consonant sounds.	
Assonance	The deliberate repetition of the same vowel sound followed by a different consonant sound.	A stitch in time saves nine.
Enjambment	Running a sentence beyond the end of a line (often runs across multiple lines) without using any punctuation.	
Imperative	An order or command to action.	
Metaphor	A comparison between two things when one thing is said to be another.	
Personification	When a non-living or non-human thing is given living or human characteristics.	
Rhyme	The repetition of words with similar sounds.	
Rhythm	The beat or pattern of stresses.	
Simile	A phrase that compares two things using 'like' or 'as'.	
Stanza	A grouping of lines in a poem similar to verses in a song.	
Verb	A doing word.	

Fairy tales

PART ONE

What are fairy tales?

A Fairy tales

In the space below, list *everything* that you associate with fairy tales including the titles of as many as you can think of.

B What are fairy tales?

Nursery rhymes:	Fables:
• basic and simple • short • rhyme • easy to remember.	• often have talking animals • have a strong moral or message.

Now that you have a definition for nursery rhymes and fables, we want you to create your own definition for fairy tales. Imagine you had to explain what fairy tales are to a child who has never heard of them before. How would you explain it?

_____

_____

_____

_____

_____

Common fairy-tale conventions:
- setting of a long time ago
- story feels like it is 'being told' to you
- a male character is on a journey or quest to rescue his princess
- a female character is always under a form of oppression (e.g. held captive)
- magic — good, evil or both.

ISBN: 9780170448826

C Categories

Sort the list of titles from Task **A** into three categories: Fairy tales, nursery rhymes and fables.

FAIRY TALES	NURSERY RHYMES	FABLES

D Word find

Find the following words in the word find:

CAPTIVE

CASTLE

ENCHANTED

EVIL

GOOD

MAGIC

OBJECT

OPPRESSION

PRINCESS

QUEST

TOWER

WITCH

JOURNEY

RESCUE

C	N	H	D	E	E	V	C	M	D	L	E	J	F	W
L	I	T	J	E	N	U	N	F	D	T	L	K	Y	I
E	V	I	T	P	A	C	C	Z	O	J	T	G	Z	T
Q	U	E	S	T	B	P	H	S	R	N	S	Z	L	C
N	A	V	X	E	B	U	E	A	E	K	A	R	M	H
R	D	Y	O	H	C	U	X	U	N	R	C	J	T	E
P	M	E	G	P	W	G	G	C	K	T	T	C	J	A
L	O	P	P	R	E	S	S	I	O	N	E	O	M	T
S	I	T	H	I	W	C	A	G	X	J	U	D	O	P
D	M	V	V	N	M	D	R	K	B	R	L	W	G	V
Y	C	P	E	C	Y	A	J	O	N	B	E	H	M	L
C	U	I	U	E	G	U	G	E	G	R	R	Z	R	L
S	M	U	P	S	B	F	Y	I	M	C	X	U	U	M
Z	Y	D	D	S	O	C	G	D	C	N	R	S	R	R
D	O	O	G	B	C	H	R	Q	A	U	O	D	C	Y

Similarities in fairy tales from around the world

PART TWO

A Cinderella

1 We're sure you all know the basic tale of 'Cinderella'. If you are unsure, work with a partner to complete this task. Communicate the story visually here in these six frames. On the lines under each frame, provide a brief description of what is happening in each picture.

1

_____
_____
_____
_____

2

_____
_____
_____
_____

3

_____
_____
_____
_____

4

_____
_____
_____

5

_____
_____
_____

6

_____
_____
_____

ISBN: 9780170448826

2 Read the following story.

The Korean Cinderella
(abridged)

Long ago in Korea, when magical creatures were as common as cabbages, there lived a child named Pear Blossom. Pear Blossom was as lovely as the pear tree planted in celebration of her birth. But one winter day, when the branches on the pear tree were still bare sticks, Pear Blossom's mother died.

"Aigo!" wailed the old man. "Who will tend to Pear Blossom now?" He put on his tall horsehair hat and went to the village matchmaker. She knew of a widow with a daughter. The girl, named Peony, was just the age of Pear Blossom.

"Three in one!" promised the matchmaker. "A wife for you and a mother and a sister for Pear Blossom." So the old gentleman took the widow for his wife.

When Omoni and Peony saw how beautiful Pear Blossom was, they were jealous of her. Omoni made her worked day and night and constantly found fault with her. And Peony was worse than no sister at all.

One day, the village was having a festival.

"Pear Blossom may go," said Omoni in a voice as sweet as barley sugar, "after she weeds the rice paddies." She handed Pear Blossom a basket of wilted turnip tops for her lunch.

"I am most grateful, Honourable Mother," said Pear Blossom. When she reached the fields, Pear Blossom dropped the basket in dismay. Rice rippled before her like a great green lake. Weeding it would take weeks.

"Who could do such a task?" she cried.

Suddenly, a whilewind twisted through the fields and a huge black ox reared up from a cloud of dust.

"DO-O-O-O" it bellowed, tossing its great horns. The ox began to munch the weeds, moving through the rows of rice faster than the wind itself. Before Pear Blossom can say "Ohhh", the whole rice field was free of weeds and yet not a single blade of rice was trampled! Pear Blossom cupped her hands over her mouth and called, "A thousand thanks!" as the ox galloped away into the horizon.

Pear Blossom hastened to the village festival. The road, which followed a crooked stream, was rough with pebbles. Pear Blossom had just slipped off one straw sandal to shake out a stone when she heard a shout.

"Make way! Make way for the magistrate!"

Four bearers, a palanquin swaying on poles across their shoulders, jogged toward her. In the chair sat a young nobleman dressed in rich robes and wearing a jade jewel in his topknot. Flustered, Pear Blossom teetered on a leg like a crane, holding her straw sandal. Her cheeks grew hot as red peppers, and she hopped behind a willow tree that grew beside the stream. As she did, her sandal splashed into the water and bobbed like a small boat, just out of reach.

"Stop!" commanded the magistrate from his palanquin. He was calling to his bearers, but Pear Blossom thought he was shouting at her, and, frightened, she fled down the road. The magistrate gazed after Pear Blossom, struck by her beauty. Then he ordered his men to fish her sandal from the stream and carry him back to the village.

At the festival, Pear Blossom forgot about her missing shoe. She watched the acrobats and tightrope walkers until she was dizzy. She swayed to the flutes and drums until her ears rang. Suddenly, she heard someone shouting at her.

"What are you doing here?" screamed her stepmother.

"I am here because a black ox ate all the weeds in the rice paddies," said Pear Blossom.

"Black ox indeed! Oxen are brown and ... " She was interrupted by the magistrate's bearers.

"Hear this!" they shouted as they elbowed the palanquin through the crowd. "We seek the girl with one shoe!"

"It's Pear Blossom!" Peony pointed at her sister. "She's lost her shoe."

The bearers put the chair down beside Pear Blossom, and the nobleman held up the straw sandal.

"The magistrate has come to arrest you," screeched the stepmother. Omoni shook Pear Blossom. "Now you will get what you deserve!"

"She must deserve me as her husband," said the magistrate, "for this lucky shoe has led me to her."

"My daughter will give you TWO shoes! That is twice as lucky!" cried Omoni. He turned to Pear Blossom and said, "I've luck enough if she who wears *this* one becomes my bride."

Pear Blossom smiled, too shy to speak, and slipped the sandal on her foot. Omoni stood staring, stiff as a statue.

When springtime came, the magistrate sent a go between to Pear Blossom's old father to arrange a grand marriage. Pear Blossom's wedding slippers were of silk, and in the courtyard of her splendid new house, a dozen pear trees bloomed.

"Ewha! Ewha!" chirruped the sparrows in the branches. That is as it was long ago, and as it should be. For, in Korea, *ewha* means "Pear Blossom."

by Shirley Climo

This is a traditional fairy tale from a very different place in the world, yet it is obviously very similar to the English version we are told.

a Why do you think they are different?

_____

_____

_____

_____

_____

b Why do you think different countries might have a fairy tale that sounds nearly identical?

_____

_____

_____

_____

_____

_____

_____

_____

_____

_____

_____

_____

 ISBN: 9780170448826

Structure of fairy tales

Fairy tales follow a simple narrative structure in that they have a beginning, a middle and an end. Usually, the characters and setting are set up in the beginning. In the middle, there is an obstacle or a conflict created. In the end, all is resolved and everyone (well, the 'goodies') live happily ever after.

Take the story of 'Hansel and Gretel', for example.

> **Beginning:** The family don't have enough food.
>
> **Middle:** Hansel and Gretel's father leaves them in the forest at his wife's insistence. The witch in the wood captures Hansel and Gretel and threatens to eat them.
>
> **End:** Hansel and Gretel escape and go home. Their stepmother has died and they forgive their father. They live happily ever after.

1 For 'The Korean Cinderella', identify the beginning, middle and end.

  a Beginning: _____
  _____
  _____
  _____
  _____
  _____
  _____

  b Middle: _____
  _____
  _____
  _____
  _____
  _____
  _____

  c End: _____
  _____
  _____
  _____
  _____
  _____
  _____

2 Creating your own fairy tale. You are now going to use what you have learned to create your own fairy tale. Part of the writing process is **planning**, so we will start there.

You need to decide what will go in the beginning, middle and end.

Beginning:	Hero	Setting	Magic object	Villain

Middle:	Obstacle 1		Obstacle 2	

End:	How are these obstacles overcome?			

 ISBN: 9780170448826

Good writers use language features to bring their writing to life and ensure that they look carefully to correct errors. The following sections will help you to practise good writing skills and teach you about language features commonly found in writing.

PART THREE

Writing skills

A ~~Speeling Spletting~~ Spelling

Each of the words in the list below is misspelt. Rewrite the word correctly in the space provided.

1 fabel _____

2 jorney _____

3 opresesion _____

4 majic _____

5 recsue _____

6 tradritional _____

7 verson _____

8 perspestive _____

9 familar _____

10 promps _____

> You may use and/or swap any of the letters from those listed here but, when you have finished, put your 'discarded' letters below. There must be only *four* letters left behind.
>
> **u p g i c i t**
>
> ____ ____ ____ ____

B The 'superhero' of the 'parts of speech' family: the verb

> A **verb** is a **doing** or action **word**: 'runs', 'went', 'made', 'fall' are all **verbs**. They tell us what someone or something did or was doing. Using verbs purposefully will help bring your writing to life.

1 Choose a verb from the list below to complete the sentences below.

lost	sing	plants	trapped
pricking	turned	enters	

a Cinderella _____ her glass slipper.

b Belle _____ the Beast's castle after he imprisons her father, Maurice.

c Rapunzel is _____ in a tower.

d The seven dwarfs _____ on the way to work.

e The wicked queen _____ her 11 stepsons into swans.

f Aurora falls asleep after _____ her finger on the spindle of a spinning wheel.

g Jack _____ bean seeds.

1 Checking with the box below, read the sentences below and write down which language technique has been used.

> **Simile:** a direct comparison between two things considered similar and always includes the words 'like' or 'as'.
>
> **Metaphor:** a comparison between two things considered similar but does not use 'like' or 'as'.
>
> **Personification:** when a non-living or non-human thing is given living or human characteristics.
>
> **Alliteration:** the repetition of consonant sounds, usually at the beginning of words, placed closely together to create a sound echo.

a The beanstalk groaned under Jack's weight. _____

b The seven dwarfs dropped down under the weight of their sacks. _____

c Rapunzel's tower was as tall as a skyscraper. _____

d Sleeping Beauty's skin is as white as snow. _____

e The moon winked at Ariel as she bobbed in the waves. _____

f Maleficent's heart was a lump of coal. _____

2 Write some descriptions about these characters using the language technique in brackets.

a The giant was enormous and had a loud voice. [metaphor]

_____

b The mice had very sharp teeth. [simile]

_____

c It was difficult to open the door to Rapunzel's room. [personification]

_____

d A description of three things Snow White did for the dwarfs. [alliteration]

_____

3 Change the sentences below from **simile** to **metaphor**.

a The eldest pig spoke as if he was as wise as an owl.

_____

b The wolf's breath smelt like a rotten barrel of grain.

_____

c Sleeping Beauty lay as still as a stone statue.

_____

d Prince Charming's heart was like a god's.

_____

   ISBN: 9780170448826

Write your own fairy tale

Using your planning from page 46 and what you have learned about writing skills, have a go at creating your own fairy tale.

If you're stuck, you can choose from the following ideas:

Characters — prince/princess/witch/wizard/giant/monster/old woman/baby/hero/knight

Settings — castle/far away/long ago/remote village/tower/cave

Magic objects — staff/jewel/cup/vase/key/ring/necklace/sword/knife/brooch/stone

Obstacles — dragon/evil tyrant/jealous mother or wife/taniwha

Animals — horse/donkey/dog/cat/frog.

Write your fairy tale here:

_____

_____

_____

_____

_____

_____

_____

_____

_____

_____

_____

_____

_____

_____

_____

_____

_____

_____

_____

_____

_____

_____

_____

ISBN: 9780170448826

Steps to revising your work

1 Reread your fairy tale from pages 49 and 50, out loud if possible.

2 With a different colour, alter any sentences that do not flow well. Are you consistent? Is your story all happening in the same tense? Does what happens to your characters make sense in the world of your story?

3 **Enriching your writing**. Circle any sentence starters that are repeated. For example, often at Year 9 many sentences start with 'Then' or 'The'.

    a Find at least three sentences that you could alter the start of. Select from the following options.
- Start by saying *when* it happened, e.g. **Later that night,** *the princess cried herself to sleep.*
- Start by saying *where* it happened, e.g. **High in her tower,** *the princess cried herself to sleep.*
- Start by saying *why* it happened, e.g. **After the door was locked**, *the princess cried herself to sleep.*
- Start with a word ending in 'ing' or 'ly' or 'ed', e.g. **Noisily**, *the princess cried herself to sleep.*

    b Write your new sentences below:

_____

_____

_____

4 Remember that verb activity we did earlier? Have a look at your story and highlight all of the verbs that you have used.

5 Choose two and look them up in a thesaurus. Find at least one synonym that would be stronger in your fairy tale.

    a Verb I have chosen: _____

      Synonyms: _____

    b Verb I have chosen: _____

      Synonyms: _____

We also talked about language features earlier: alliteration, simile, metaphor, personification.

6 **Reread your writing**. Did you use any of these to bring your story to life? Highlight them if so. If not, add in at least one. This will make your writing more interesting for the reader. You may decide to type your story on a device at this stage to make editing easier.

7 **Editing**. After you have revised your work (sometimes multiple times), you will edit your piece to get it ready for publication. This is where we look at the surface features and check:
- spelling
- grammar
- sentence structure
- vocabulary
- opening
- closing.

At this stage, it can be good to get a friend or an adult to check over your work. Sometimes you can't see your own mistakes.

PART FOUR

Close-up on some ~~tails~~ tales!

A 'The Three Little Pigs'

We're sure you know the traditional tale of 'The Three Little Pigs'.

1 Fill in the left-hand side of the chart below with what you know (think about the conventions from page 40).
2 Then search for the YouTube video of 'The True Story of The Three Little Pigs!' by Jon Scieszka, watch it and fill in the right-hand side.

TRADITIONAL VERSION	JON SCIESZKA'S VERSION

3 Which version do you prefer? Why?

_____

_____

_____

4 Point of view (POV)

In this retelling of 'The Three Little Pigs', the author changes the point of view of the story. Usually readers sympathise with the pigs. Here, readers hear the wolf's side of the story. Complete this sentence:

I think _____ is telling the truth because _____

_____

_____

5 Write a letter below to one of the characters in 'The True Story of The Three Little Pigs!' by Jon Scieszka. Give the character some good advice.

B Different perspectives (POV's)

Now you have read a different version of 'The Three Little Pigs', think about how other fairy tales could be different if told from another point of view.

1 Use the space below to rewrite a story from a different perspective. Choose from this list or come up with your own idea:

- Cinderella's stepsisters
- The wolf in 'Little Red Riding Hood'
- The giant in 'Jack and the Beanstalk'
- Snow White's stepmother
- The witch in 'Hansel and Gretel'
- The beast from 'Beauty and the Beast'.

Planning:

Now start writing:

_____
_____
_____
_____
_____
_____
_____
_____
_____
_____
_____
_____
_____
_____
_____

 ISBN: 9780170448826

2 All cultures around the world have fairy tales.

a Find a copy of a fairy tale you are not familiar with from your school library, local library, or find one on the internet.

b Read the story and then create a book report by completing the following prompts. Answer the last three questions in complete sentences.

- Fairy tale title
- Author
- Illustrator
- Country of origin
- Setting
- Main characters
- What was the conflict or problem in this fairy tale?
- What did the main character have to do in order to overcome the problem?
- Conclusion: How did the fairy tale end?

 ISBN: 9780170448826

3 Enter and exit the maze and, as you journey through, collect the letters that will *spell the name* of the famous brothers who published folklore and popularised traditional oral tales like 'Cinderella', 'The Frog Prince' and 'Rapunzel'.

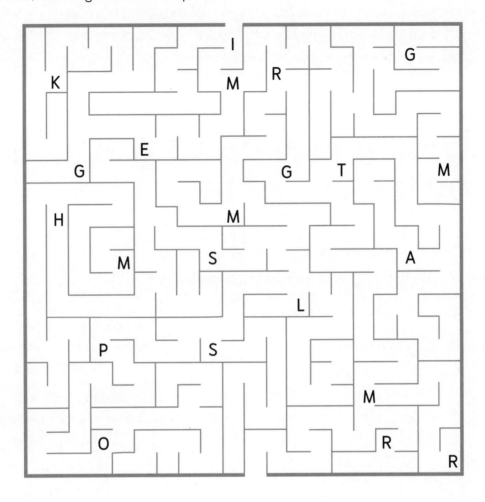

Write your 'collected' letters here: _____

Write the answer here: _____

4 Solve these anagrams. The words below, when their letters are reordered, become the characters from famous fairy tales. The answers could be one, two or three words, but you must use all the letters. The number in the brackets tells you how many words.

a   cleaner lid _____ [1]

b   two whines _____ [2]

c   zen up lar _____ [1]

d   reglet _____ [1]

e   baste _____ [1]

f   tangi _____ [1]

g   pincer _____ [1]

h   eight pellet hitters _____ [4]

i   bald fig bow _____ [3]

j   unsplit elm skirt _____ [1]

I have something to say

We all have something to say, every day, and sometimes the opportunity arises to make yourself heard. It is a good idea to learn how to speak and write your opinion so that when the time comes, you will be listened to.

PART ONE Using words to get others to listen

 A Identifying techniques used to persuade

1 Mix and match the following terms with the correct definition.

Persuade (noun: persuasion)	A short account of a particular incident or event, especially of an interesting or amusing nature.
Anecdote	Specific words chosen to evoke a certain emotion in the reader/listener.
Personal pronouns	To induce to believe by appealing to reason or understanding; to convince.
Emotive language	To say or utter again.
Repeat (noun: repetition)	Words that stand in place of nouns (names).

2 Fill in the blanks with the correct term from the table above.

a I used _____ _____ in my speech to connect with my audience.

b To emphasise how scared my character was, I used _____.

c To make my writing seem sad, my teacher suggested I use more _____ _____.

d We could not _____ him to wait.

e The speaker told us an _____ about her time in Fiji when she fell off a jetty.

ISBN: 9780170448826

3 This is a short opinion piece that uses the techniques from the table on page 58. Read it through carefully.

To the principal of Mountain High School

I am writing to you to register my concerns about the way seniors crowd the tuck shop during break times here at Mountain High School. I am a current Year 9 student and I, as well as most of my cohort, find this situation unbearable. Starting at a new, large school can be hard, and being scared to line up to buy food does not help with this. Food is important for learning because without fuel, our brains don't work.

Although I queue as per instructions, Year 12 and Year 13 students crowd in around me, jostling me and pushing their way ahead of me. They reach over me, shout out instructions and generally leave me feeling unsafe. I thought that school was meant to be a safe place for all? I know, I know, you could say that I don't have to use the tuck shop. However, it is a school facility provided for all students and staff to access and I believe it is your duty to make sure it is a safe place.

My suggestion for fixing this problem is for there to be a dedicated Year 9 line created at the tuck shop. We currently have three lines (cash only; cash + eftpos; eftpos only). It would be easy to rename one of these lines the Year 9 line.

Please also find attached the results from the survey I did of the Year 9 cohort about this issue. You will see from the results of this that I am not the only one who feels this way.

I look forward to hearing from you,

A concerned Year 9 student from Mountain High School.

Label the highlighted parts of the text with the correct technique from the table on page 58.

a _____

b _____

c _____

d _____

e _____

B How to get your opinion across

The best pieces of persuasive writing follow a simple structure that helps get your opinion across. Firstly, you make it clear **who** you are. This will help the reader/listener figure out why you might have an interest in this topic (people who have an interest in an issue and are affected by it are called stakeholders). You then need to clearly state **what the problem is (why this is a problem)**.

Good persuasive writers then follow up the problem by proposing a solution. If you don't provide a solution, you are just complaining about something, you are not being persuasive that things need to change.

1 Read over the opinion piece again and identify the following.

a Who is writing this piece: _____

b What the problem is: _____

c What the proposed solution is: _____

2 The proposed solution isn't really ideal. What problems can you see with the solution? What do you think are some alternatives to fix this issue?

_____

_____

_____

_____

_____

3 Your turn. Write a formal persuasive letter to the school council or to your principal using the _same_ structure as the letter on page 59. Think about:
- what you want
- why it is needed
- how to appeal to the reader
- suggestions/solutions offered.

You may wish to plan your draft on a separate piece of paper.

_____

_____

_____

_____

_____

_____

_____

_____

_____

_____

_____

_____

_____

_____

_____

_____

_____

_____

_____

_____

_____

_____

_____

ISBN: 9780170448826

Looking at visual language used to communicate

PART TWO

A Image one

Look at this visual image below and note the range of visual and persuasive language techniques used to communicate the message.

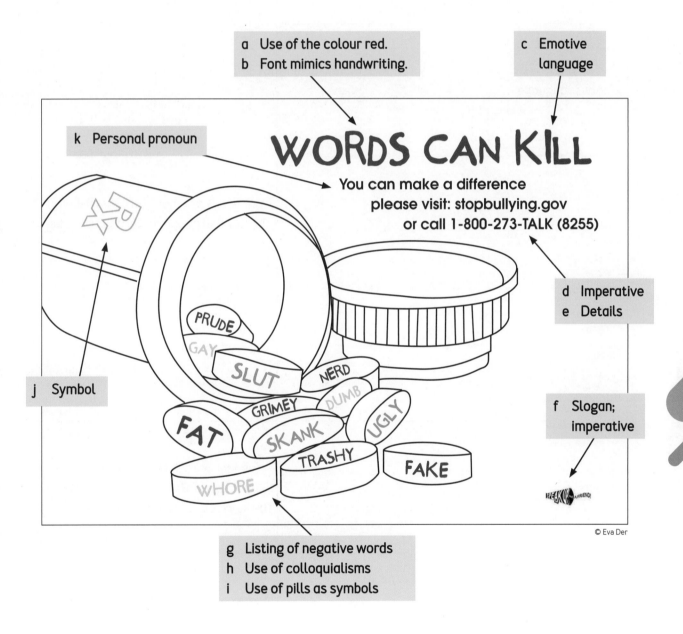

a Use of the colour red.
b Font mimics handwriting.

c Emotive language

k Personal pronoun

WORDS CAN KILL

You can make a difference
please visit: stopbullying.gov
or call 1-800-273-TALK (8255)

d Imperative
e Details

j Symbol

f Slogan;
imperative

g Listing of negative words
h Use of colloquialisms
i Use of pills as symbols

© Eva Der

1 Complete the table below which explains the effect of each technique identified and its purpose. If you are unsure of the definition of any of the words, look back through this book or check out the glossary at the back. We have completed the first one for you:

TECHNIQUE USED	EFFECT	PURPOSE
Colour red	Red is the colour of blood, so makes us think of death.	The colour and font is like in a horror movie when the killer writes a message of warning.
Handwriting font	Personalises it — as if the person is in a hurry because time is running out.	
Emotive language		
Imperative		Commands are more forceful, usually shorter and people naturally try to be compliant.
Details		
Slogan		A familiar phrase that is easily identified by others and summarises the key ideas of the message.
Listing		Addresses any questions or gaps as to what might be included or affected by the action/message.

   ISBN: 9780170448826

TECHNIQUE USED	EFFECT	PURPOSE
Colloquialism	Information language that attempts to mimic a conversation between friends.	The viewers/listeners are more likely to take in the message if they feel the speaker is speaking at 'their level' and/or as friends — makes it informal.
Symbolism	Directly relates one idea (often well known) to the idea being communicated so that the listener or viewer can understand the message.	
Symbol	Easily identifiable idea.	
Personal pronoun	Immediately draws the reader/listener into the communication because the message is being spoken directly at the person receiving the message; can also make everyone feel included in the communication.	

2 What did the creator of this visual image want to say?

_____

_____

_____

3 Why is the choice of the nasty words on the 'pills' an effective choice?

_____

_____

_____

4 What action should we take as a result of viewing this image?

_____

_____

_____

Look at the visual image below and do the tasks that follow.

1 Label the name of the language feature identified in each speech box. Refer to the chart on pages 62 and 63 and/or the glossary if you need help.

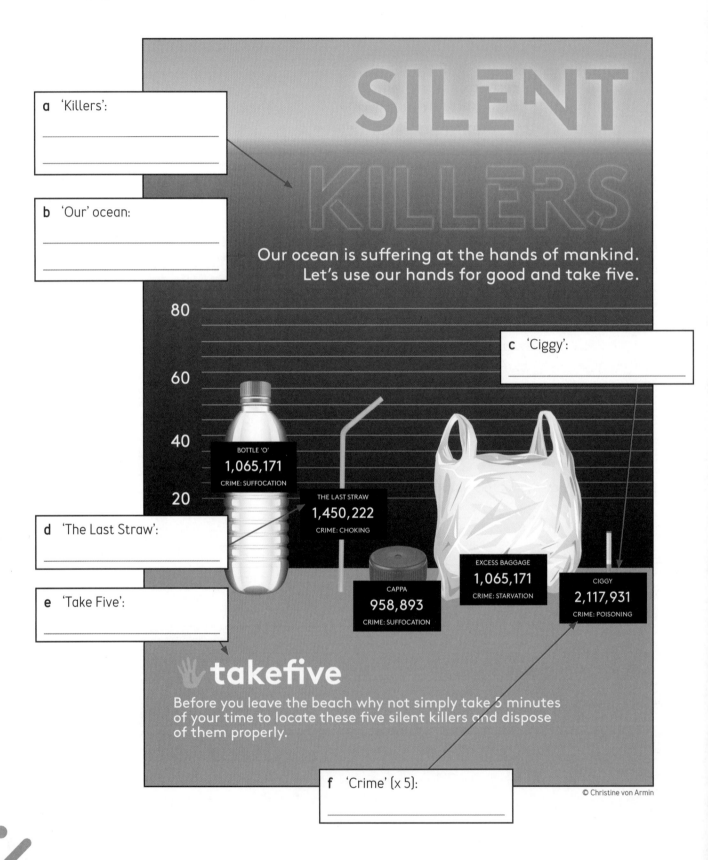

a 'Killers':
_____
_____

b 'Our' ocean:
_____
_____

c 'Ciggy':
_____

d 'The Last Straw':
_____

e 'Take Five':
_____

f 'Crime' (x 5):
_____

SILENT KILLERS

Our ocean is suffering at the hands of mankind. Let's use our hands for good and take five.

BOTTLE 'O'
1,065,171
CRIME: SUFFOCATION

THE LAST STRAW
1,450,222
CRIME: CHOKING

CAPPA
958,893
CRIME: SUFFOCATION

EXCESS BAGGAGE
1,065,171
CRIME: STARVATION

CIGGY
2,117,931
CRIME: POISONING

takefive
Before you leave the beach why not simply take 5 minutes of your time to locate these five silent killers and dispose of them properly.

© Christine von Armin

 ISBN: 9780170448826

2 What does this poster want us to do?

_____

_____

3 Why should we do this?

_____

_____

4 Designers often use a 'visual metaphor' to help develop their ideas. A metaphor compares two things. In this visual, the two things that are being compared are the conventions of a 'police line-up' and 'crimes' committed by rubbish.

Why do you think the creator of this poster chose this metaphor?

_____

_____

5 List one example from image two for each of the following:

a emotive language

_____

b an imperative

_____

c use of repetition

_____

d pun/play on words

_____

e colloquial language

_____

f use of graphics

_____

g use of colour

_____

6 Choose two techniques from above and explain how they help us to understand the message.

NAME OF TECHNIQUE	DETAIL	REASON USED

Make your own poster

Choose from one of the following topics or any other idea that is important to you: animal rights, climate change, child poverty, clean school bathrooms, school uniforms, discrimination, state of our water, tourism, gangs, drugs, bullying, promoting an event, ...

1 What do you want people to know?

_____

_____

2 Why do you want them to know this?

_____

_____

3 What do you want them to do as a result of viewing your poster (also known as 'call to action')?

_____

_____

4 What do you think might be the outcome of this 'call to action'?

_____

_____

5 How will you use verbal and visual techniques to communicate your message? Use the table below to help you plan your visual image. We have given you an example.

MESSAGE/IDEA	TECHNIQUE	DESCRIPTION/DETAIL	INTENDED EFFECT AND REASON FOR USING THIS
There is hope if we look after our environment	Use of colour	A single green leaf growing up from black soil	Green represents growth and the promise of life; the green contrasts with the black of the soil, which represents death

 ISBN: 9780170448826

6 Use the space below to draft out your design.

1 Match the terms in the box below with the definitions in the table. We have provided two answers to get you started.

cliché	hyperbole	imperative	jargon
layout	metaphor	neologism	pun
personification	repetition	simile	symbol
rhyme	rhetorical question		

TERM	DEFINITION
Symbol	An image/picture that represents an idea.
	Ordering or commanding an action.
	A phrase that compares two things, using 'like' or 'as'.
	An exaggeration.
	When a non-living or non-human thing is given living or human characteristics.
	Specialised language used by people who work or share a common interest.
Cliché	An overused expression.
	An expression that plays on different meanings of the same word or phrase.
	The use of words with similar sounds.
	A comparison between two things where one thing is said to be another.
	Words or statements used more than once for effect.
	A question in which an answer is not expected (asked to involve the audience).
	The arrangement of words and pictures on a page.
	New or made-up words.

2 Below is a crossword of visual language features you should be familiar with. Refer to the glossary if you need help.

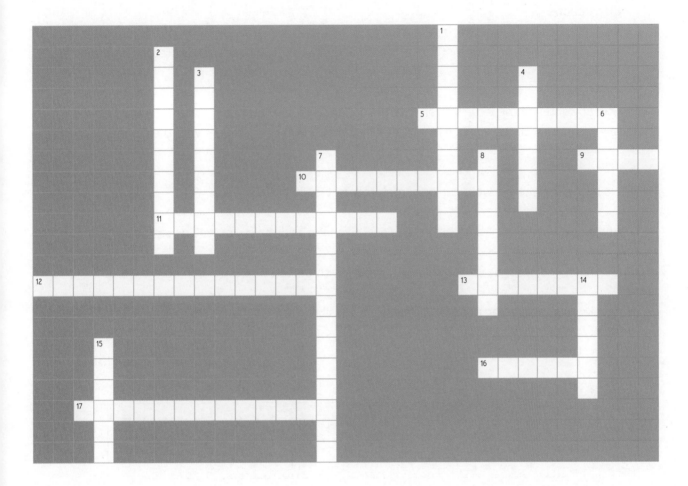

ACROSS

5 Reliable data used to support a point.

9 The style of the lettering used in an image.

10 A command or call to action.

11 Repetition of consonant sounds draws attention to important words.

12 Used to involve the audience. (2 words)

13 To compare in order to show differences.

16 An image of something which represents an idea.

17 The largest visual image which the viewer sees first. (2 words)

DOWN

1 A word or phrase said again for emphasis.

2 The type of question that does not require an answer and makes your audience think.

3 Exaggeration.

4 A series of words or phrases linked together in a meaningful group.

6 A catchy phrase.

7 Words and ideas designed to evoke strong feelings in a person. (2 words)

8 A comparison but saying one thing 'is' the other.

14 Comparing two things as being similar using 'like' or 'as'.

15 How the words and images are organised on the image.

3 'I have something to say' vocabulary code cracker.

Instructions:

Each number in the crossword cell (on page 71) represents a different letter of the alphabet. All of the words are from this section, i.e. the vocabulary and techniques associated with persuasive language.

Start by entering the letters given: in every square with the number 2, write the letter O, and in every square with the number 12, write the letter C, and in every square with the number 13, write the letter L.

Now look for where a word can be completed. This is the starter word.

Enter new letters into the appropriate squares on the grids below as well as on the puzzle.

Go ahead and fill in the corresponding numbers with the letters in your completed word.

Stuck? Think of spelling patterns; think of the possible word from this section that might fit. Really stuck? Have a peek at the answers to get you going again. Use a pencil and fill in the boxes below to help you see which letters are left.

1	2	3	4	5	6	7	8	9	10	11	12	13
	O										C	L

14	15	16	17	18	19	20	21	22	23	24	25	26

> Write the number below the letters of the alphabet. This will help you work out what letters are still to be used.

A	B	C	D	E	F	G	H	I	J	K	L	M
		12									13	

N	O	P	Q	R	S	T	U	V	W	X	Y	Z
	2											

 ISBN: 9780170448826

Feeling frightened

Horror is one of the most popular genres in writing. Fear is a powerful emotion and often horror stories are designed to terrify you. In this section, we will look at powerful horror writing and unpack how the writers build a sense of fear in their reader.

But first, what is the horror genre?

PART
ONE

 A What do you know?

1   Use this space to brainstorm everything you associate with the horror genre. This could include the names of written texts or films that you know of. Think about what has made these texts scary.

Common attributes of the horror genre:
- An attempt to make the audience experience fright, fear or disgust.
- The stories often involve an evil force, event or supernatural character.
- Settings are usually in small towns, in quiet neighbourhoods and in woods.
- Shadows and darkness play an important part.
- The colour red is often symbolic.
- Often the characters in danger are children or young adults.

2 Below are 12 of the most iconic scary movie quotes. Select the correct word from the list below to complete the quote. Hint: test an adult to see how well they know these famous horror films.

Johnny	alive	dead	better	boat	here
mother	play	scream	scary	asleep	afraid

a 'I see _____ people.' *The Sixth Sense*

b 'Heeere's _____!' *The Shining*

c 'You're gonna need a bigger _____.' *Jaws*

d 'It's _____!' *Frankenstein*

e 'Do you like _____ movies?' *Scream*

f 'They're _____!' *Poltergeist*

g 'Do you want to _____ a game?'" *Saw*

h 'A boy's best friend is his _____.' *Psycho*

i 'Sometimes dead is _____.' *Pet Sematary*

j 'Be afraid, be very _____.' *The Fly*

k 'Whatever you do, don't fall _____.' *A Nightmare on Elm Street*

l 'In space, no one can hear you _____.' *Alien*

3 Match the words on the left with the correct antonyms on the right.

a approach   good, undamaged, pristine, healthy

b problem   fearless, brave, daring, courageous

c abandoned   warm, fervid, scorching, boiling

d darkness   withdraw, depart, go, retreat

e terrified   solution, resolution, answer, advantage

f isolate   light, brightness, daylight, brilliance

g dilapidated   adopted, supported, defended, cherished

h rotten   calm, cheer, assurance, security

i terror   connect, unite, attach, combine

j cold   fresh, sweet, trustworthy, wholesome

Setting the scene

Some of the common features of horror writing:

- Use of sense impressions to build up the picture — sights, sounds and smells to create tension.
- Powerful verbs.
- Use of words to suggest decay, abandonment and isolation.
- Short simple sentence for clarity and dramatic impact.
- Often ends on a dramatic cliffhanger.
- Complex words for extra layers of meaning.
- Use of darkness and cold to build suspense.
- Symbols — often of death (crow, gravestone, black cat, abandoned house, dead trees, night-time).

Good writers use a specific setting to help them develop characters, plot and themes.

1 Read the following extract.

> The pit had been dug three days before the start of the battle. It was between two squat boulders, the earth pale and sandy, littered with small stones, sharp rocks and bits of bleached bone.
>
> Half in the earth and half in the air — those were Hecate's instructions. An equal measure of each opposing ingredient: living and dead, beginning and ending. Black and white. Smooth and rough.
>
> All night they had sat around the smoking fire of the hideout, waiting.
>
> First, for the girl with blood on her hands.
>
> Second, for the offering.
>
> Third, for the alarm.
>
> They passed between them the cup of potion that kept their minds alert and their bodies awake. It was not long before she arrived, the bleating cries of her cargo muffled by sack and binding. The albino admitted the girl, and the shorn one took the newborn, untied the string that held the neck of the bag tight, peered in and grinned, her blackened and stubby teeth glistening against the sharp light of the fire.
>
> Their visitor untied her cloak, revealing lad's breeks and a coarse, muddy shirt.
>
> 'Is it unhurt?' the girl asked the women.
>
> 'It is alive, healthy and perfect for our purposes. You have done well, Sister Breanna,' the witch said, cackling and huffing as she carried the bag to the edge of their circle.
>
> *from* Birthright *by T.K. Roxborogh*

2 Answer the following questions and give evidence from the extract above.

    a Where is the action set?

    _____

    Evidence from the text:

    _____

b What time period do you think it is?

_____

Evidence from the text:

_____

c What is the season and time of day?

_____

Evidence from the text:

_____

d What sights, sounds, smells and textures are described?

_____

Evidence from the text:

_____

To understand the setting of the story, we can ask some basic questions. The answers to these questions might be direct (telling) or indirect (showing) writing.

- A **direct description** is stated clearly and tells us what is going on/when it is, etc.
- An **indirect description** gives clues for the reader to read between the lines (infer) what the details are. This is often called 'showing, not telling'. For example; 'She looked up at the stars' lets us know the time of the day in a more interesting way than just being told it is night-time.

3 Write down two examples of _direct_ description in the extract. Identify the things being described.

a _____

_____

_____

b _____

_____

_____

4 Write down two examples of _indirect_ description in the extract. Explain what the information is telling us.

a _____

_____

_____

b _____

_____

_____

C Character development

Let's look at how Roald Dahl has created the character of Mary Maloney in the short story 'Lamb to the Slaughter'. You can read the full short story at: https://www.classicshorts.com/stories/lamb.html

> The room was warm and clean, the curtains drawn, the two table lamps alight — hers and the one by the empty chair opposite. On the sideboard behind her, two tall glasses, soda water, whiskey. Fresh ice cubes in the Thermos bucket.
>
> Mary Maloney was waiting for her husband to come home from work.
>
> Now and again she would glance up at the clock, but without anxiety, merely to please herself with the thought that each minute gone by made it nearer the time when he would come. There was a slow smiling air about her, and about everything she did.

1 What are your first impressions of Mary Maloney?

_____

_____

2 How has Dahl made you feel this way about her?

_____

_____

When Mary's husband gets home, he tells her that he has had an affair and that he is leaving her, even though she is six months pregnant with their child. This part of the story explains Mary's reaction.

> When she walked across the room she couldn't feel her feet touching the floor. She couldn't feel anything at all — except a slight nausea and a desire to vomit. Everything was automatic now — down the steps to the cellar, the light switch, the deep freeze, the hand inside the cabinet taking hold of the first object it met. She lifted it out, and looked at it. It was wrapped in paper, so she took off the paper and looked at it again.
>
> A leg of lamb.
>
> All right then, they would have lamb for supper. She carried it upstairs, holding the thin bone-end of it with both her hands, and as she went through the living-room, she saw him standing over by the window with his back to her, and she stopped.
>
> "For God's sake," he said, hearing her, but not turning round. "Don't make supper for me. I'm going out."
>
> At that point, Mary Maloney simply walked up behind him and without any pause she swung the big frozen leg of lamb high in the air and brought it down as hard as she could on the back of his head.
>
> She might just as well have hit him with a steel club.
>
> She stepped back a pace, waiting, and the funny thing was that he remained standing there for at least four or five seconds, gently swaying. Then he crashed to the carpet.

   ISBN: 9780170448826

In this story, Dahl has taken us by surprise as we didn't think the calm, gentle and pregnant Mrs Maloney could kill her husband, but it quickly becomes clear what she is capable of.

> It was extraordinary, now, how clear her mind became all of a sudden. She began thinking very fast. As the wife of a detective, she knew quite well what the penalty would be...
>
> She carried the meat into the kitchen, placed it in a pan, turned the oven on high, and shoved it inside. Then she washed her hands and ran upstairs to the bedroom... She tried a smile. It came out rather peculiar. She tried again.
>
> "Hullo, Sam," she said brightly, aloud.
>
> The voice sounded peculiar too.
>
> "I want some potatoes please, Sam. Yes, and I think a can of peas."
>
> That was better. Both the smile and the voice were coming out better now. She rehearsed it several times more. Then she ran downstairs, took her coat, went out the back door, down the garden, into the street.
>
> It wasn't six o'clock yet and the lights were still on in the grocery shop.
>
> "Hullo, Sam," she said brightly, smiling at the man behind the counter.

3 How did Mary kill her husband?

_____

4 How did she get rid of the murder weapon?

_____

5 What did she do to ensure that she had an alibi for the time of death?

_____

_____

_____

6 How has your opinion of Mary Maloney changed from question 1?

_____

_____

_____

7 Did Dahl catch you by surprise with what happened? How did he do this, do you think?

_____

_____

_____

_____

_____

_____

How to write a response (long answer)

A crucial skill in English is being able to respond to a question, using evidence to back up your comments. We will use an acronym to help you remember what should go into a paragraph:

T – topic sentence

E – evidence

E – explanation

P – personal response (I think/I learned/this made me realise/this made me value).

For the next task, you could choose any text you wish to complete the work below. If stuck, you can use Mary Maloney.

Your question is:

Describe an **important character** in the text and **explain** why they are important.

1   Your first paragraph is going to *describe* the character.

   a   Write down *one* statement about the character. This will be your *topic sentence*.

   _____

   _____

   b   Now provide *one* example from the story that is *evidence* to prove this statement. Include the context (whereabouts in the story/what is happening). If you can, also include a relevant *quote*.

   _____

   _____

   _____

   c   Explain what the quote and example mean and how they *prove* your topic sentence. This will be your *explanation*.

   _____

   _____

   _____

   _____

   d   Write the *purpose* of description we are given by the author; provide a one- or two-sentence key lesson we the audience learn from this observation about the character. This is where you describe what it is we are to learn, know and/or understand about the character *and* perhaps about the world from seeing this detail.

   _____

   _____

   _____

   _____

   _____

   _____

   _____

   _____

2 Your second paragraph is going to *explain* why this character is important.

   a Write down *one* reason the character is important to the story *or* something we learn from the character. This will be your *topic sentence*.

     _____

     _____

   b Now provide *one* example from the text that is *evidence* to prove this statement. Include the context (whereabouts in the story/what is happening). If you can, also include a relevant *quote*.

     _____

     _____

     _____

     _____

   c Explain what the quote and example mean and how they *prove* your topic sentence. This will be your *explanation*.

     _____

     _____

     _____

     _____

   d Write the *purpose* of description we are given by the author; provide a one- or two-sentence key lesson we the audience learn from this observation about the character. This is where you describe what it is we are to learn, know and/or understand about the character *and* perhaps about the world from seeing this detail.

     _____

     _____

     _____

     _____

     _____

     _____

     _____

> Well done! You have created a great long answer. If you were to pull all of the answers together and add an introduction and conclusion, you would have an essay. Essay writing is a crucial skill in Senior English.

We are now going to give you some 'ingredients' of a story for you to choose how your story will go. This is what is known as a 'pick a plot' or 'pick a path' story.

Pick a path for your own horror story

PART TWO

A Select some key elements to your story

1 Character.
  a Your main (point of view) character. Circle one from each column.

Age	Occupation	Favourite pastime	Hates	Greatest fear
19 years old	apprentice electrician	surfing	disorder	blood
24 years old	computer programmer	listening to music	loud noises	water
35 years old	nurse	knitting	being late	small spaces
52 years old	gardener	cooking	letting people down	spiders
79 years old	dog walker	playing pool	pain	heights

  b Your character's internal goal is to avoid discomfort. Choose your character's external goal or 'object of desire'.

  to make the perfect meal   to impress the boss   to make someone jealous

  to get through the evening without making a fool of oneself

2 Setting the scene.
  a Start of the story. Your character is in the kitchen: what type of kitchen is it? Circle your choices.

  modern   run-down   family kitchen   cluttered

  tidy   clean   dirty   small   spacious

  b Preparing a meal for … Circle your choice.

  the boss   a date   family members   a favourite rock band

  c Circle one of the following dishes to make.

  guacamole   apple crumble   fish pie   homemade fries

  cheese on toast   fresh vegetable salad

  d You must also use at least one of the following. Circle what you will use.

  a lemon   a lime   tabasco sauce   chilli powder   vinegar   salt

  And, you must use a knife.

 ISBN: 9780170448826

3 Inciting incident (the event that will set your character on the path to action).

   a Choose one of the following (or make up your own).

- A dish catches fire, burning the character.
- Someone drops and breaks a precious heirloom bowl. The main character is stabbed by a shard.
- There are maggots/weta/crawling insects in the food. The main character tries to kill them by crushing with a small kitchen mallet but misses and hits his/her hand/fingers instead.
- The knife slips and injures the main character.
- Water is spilt on the floor and the character twists his/her ankle or breaks a toe.
- _____ *(your idea)*

   b In one or two sentences, describe how the event happens, how your character reacts/feels, and what he/she does to fix the problem (remember what the internal goal is). This is the plot outline to your horror story.

_____

_____

_____

_____

_____

   c Share your summary with a friend. Does he/she have any questions? Does he/she foresee any problems? Does he/she have suggestions? Write notes here.

_____

_____

_____

_____

_____

B Write the draft of your story

You will have a chance to come back and edit but, for now, follow the outline and character details you have selected on the previous pages. Choose from one of the following starter sentences which fits with the planning work you have done for Task **A** or make up one of your own. You will write your story on the following pages.

Story starters:

i The oven was to blame.

ii It looked like it was going to turn out perfectly.

iii A little blood never hurt anyone.

iv It was my first time doing this on my own.

v I had a bad feeling right from the start.

vi _____ *(your choice)*

ISBN: 9780170448826

Time to put your story to one side to 'rest'. You will come back to it again to rework it.

   ISBN: 9780170448826

A horror example

Read this horror story by Tania Roxborogh, then do the tasks that follow.

Thirty-six hours

The numbers on the wall clock flip over to 5:45. Fifteen minutes until The Boss is expected with the others for dinner. The roast chicken comes out of the oven in ten minutes, to rest before being served. The table places are precisely set. The guacamole, the only thing left to make: onion, lemon juice, tabasco sauce, avocado, a pinch of salt.

He scoops the avocado out of its skin and dumps the flesh into a bowl. In goes the chopped onion, salt and a splash of tabasco sauce. The last ingredient is the lemon juice. He holds the yellow fruit with his long, pale fingers arched, the tips tucked safely away from the edge of the knife, but, just as he slices down on the lemon, there is a bang bang bang: he jumps, the knife slips, slicing a deep cut into his left forefinger.

Someone is at the front door.

Blood swells up from the wound and he drops the knife on the chopping board. Bang, Bang. The loud knocking again. His visitors are too early. He looks at his hand, the blood now flowing easily down the finger and onto the lemon, the chopping block and knife. He picks up the slice of lemon but the clear, tart juice drips into the cut on his finger stinging like white hot fire.

'You home?' a voice calls from the other side of the door.

For a moment, he is uncertain which thing to do first: answer the question, stop the bleeding, finish making the dish. He chooses the finger, but, as he reaches over the bench to retrieve a tea-towel, three great drops of dark blood plop into the guacamole mixture. He grabs the towel, wraps it tightly around his hand, the stain of red quickly spreading through the cloth and goes to the front door.

Despite the bone biting pain in his finger, the lemon juice still stinging the edges, he inhales deeply, opens the door and greets his guests.

'The guacamole is delicious,' The Boss says, smearing a great dollop onto a cracker. 'What's the special ingredient?'

As if in answer, the throbbing in his finger swells, the pounding of his heart answering the regular throb of the wound.

'How's the cut?' the other guest asks. 'Looks like you made a bit of mess of yourself.'

The bloodied knife remains on the chopping board; the large drops of blood still make a trail over the bench toward the neat stack of tea-towels. The stained cloth has been replaced by a respectable Footrot Flats plaster though it does nothing to stop the burning sting of the lemon juice working itself into the deep cut.

'Fine,' he lies. 'I've forgotten about it.'

Afterwards, he cannot face the dishes and his guests did not offer to do them. His finger is still sore and it crosses his mind that maybe there was some kind of bacteria on the blade or something wrong with the lemon — the juice was particularly tart. He pulls down the first aid box from above the fridge. He examines the expiry date on the tube of anti-bacterial cream and frowns. Past its 'use by' date. It goes into the bin.

Carefully, he pulls off the plaster but immediately the bright red blood springs up along the line of the wound and a deep aching, like bruising, thrums along the bones in his thumb and forearm. Not a good sign.

Continued over page.

He re-dresses the wound, takes two Panadol and carries the glass to his room.

Changing into his pajamas is difficult because the buttons of his shirt are uncooperative with the bandaged hand. By the time he gets himself under the covers, he shivers with cold, exhaustion, and pain.

The alarm clock does not wake him. The entire night he felt his blood pulse around his body — set off from the ache in his hand. He rises, body stiff, head thick with lack of sleep and checks his finger. Blood has seeped through the bandage but it is dark and dried — a good sign. Again, he carefully peels off the old plaster. This time, no fresh blood springs up. The edges around the thin cut are angry red so perhaps a few minutes of air would be good for the healing process.

The row of work shirts hang, un-ironed, in his wardrobe. He selects Wednesday's shirt: a pale blue cotton one worn only twice before. While he waits for the iron to heat up, he goes into the kitchen to make coffee but is greeted with the sight of last night's unwashed dishes and bloody mishap. His appetite for coffee disappears.

There is a satisfying pleasure in erasing the creases and crinkles of things not perfect, like this shirt; like his life. He flips the shirt over and starts up the right arm but, maybe because he is tired, maybe because he is out of balance, or maybe the extra care he is taking with his finger changed the rhythm: the hot iron knocks hard into his left forefinger, burning like a dog bite so he falls back with a yelp. The iron drops to the floor, sparking, creating a sharp popping sound from the socket and puffing out grey-white smoke. He grabs for the cord and yanks out the plug but adding another sickening wave of pain to his hand.

He slides down the wall, holding his hand in front of him: the bleeding has started again: bright, red blood and, beside the cut, the skin is scorched white and red, a blister already swelling over the damaged flesh. On the floor rests Wednesday's shirt — a reminder the day was still a work day. He grabs the shirt — most of it was ironed so it should be okay but, as he puts it on, sees that there are large blood stains on the sleeve.

'Hard night, last night, eh?' the office junior smirks. 'Or did you forget where you put your iron?'

The young worker's snarky observation about his current state of dress is nothing in comparison to the nerve-screeching irritation of the regular drum beat of pain and ache in his head. 'Both,' he mutters in reply and heads for the office first aid tin — for more painkillers and fresh anti-bacterial cream for he was certain now that the cut is septic and he is at risk of developing septicaemia. The tube of cream is new, and the plasters are hospital grade, which is a good sign. The white salve soothes the heat and sting of the wound and gives him hope that his day will improve.

But, by the time he's re-covered the finger, the pounding beat of his heart and the gooush gooush gooush sound of blood circulating through his body grows louder with each passing hour so that, by the time he drags himself through his front door, he is sick with anxiety and fear and utterly exhausted.

That night, he lies in bed unable to sleep, unable to think of anything other than what might be the outcome if indeed his finger has become infected with some type of antibiotic-resistant bug. He'd read it takes only thirty-six hours for the body to show symptoms. He'd read a news article about a particularly nasty outbreak in a hospital down country. Hadn't someone from the office been visiting relatives in that town?

   ISBN: 9780170448826

The painkillers weren't working; the mindfulness meditation — he never did that right anyway — was no good. It was certain the hand was infected and the poison now travelling up his arm. It was only a matter of time before it got to his heart and then his brain.

He slides out of bed and pads into the kitchen. The light above the bench reveals a mise en scène of some horror movie. The knife, the culprit, the cause of his agony, lies sedately where he left if thirty-six hours ago. He picks it up with his right hand, the cool wooden handle comfortable in his grip. He spreads his left hand on the chopping board, the left finger swollen, hot, red; the long thin cut oozing clear liquid. He looks at the blade and then at this finger. His head pounds, his mouth is dry.

Outside, a neighbour, as is her custom, is walking her dog. She stops when she sees the light go on in the house of the strange young man who lives alone there. His curtains are open and she can see clearly as he stands, looking down, frowning. The dog comes to sit at her feet. They both look up at the man in the window. They see the large knife in his hand and see him raise it high above his head. They watch as he brings it down fast, slamming the blade into the object on the board.

The neighbour gasps. The young man screams. The numbers on the wall clock flop over to 5:45.

by T.K. Roxborogh ©

1 Write down what you think is the very next thing that happens.

_____

_____

_____

_____

2 Think back over your own 'pick a path' guidelines and answer the following questions.

a What was the character's external goal/object of desire?

_____

_____

b How is the scene set?

_____

_____

c What was the inciting incident?

_____

_____

d How did he go about ensuring he was safe from pain?

_____

_____

3 In the chart below, the list on the right are the steps the author takes to push the character to his actions at the end of the story. However, they are all jumbled up. Reorganise them so that they are in the right order by putting the letter which goes with the sentence on the left.

Events of 'Thirty-six Hours' in the correct order		Events listed out of order	
1	q	a	Anti-bacterial cream has expired
2		b	Burns his finger on the iron
3		c	Slices finger with knife
4		d	Blood on his shirt
5		e	Guests come early
6		f	Gets more painkillers and fresh anti-bacterial cream
7		g	Doesn't sleep
8		h	Kitchen is a mess from the night before
9		i	A second night without sleep
10		j	Blood in the guacamole
11		k	Pain is unbearable
12	f	l	Fearful the infection is going to travel to his heart and brain
13		m	Fears his wound is infected
14		n	Read about a septicaemia outbreak in a nearby town
15		o	Lemon juice in the cut
16		p	Returns to the kitchen to remove the cause of his pain
17		q	Making dinner
18		r	Work colleague teases him for his appearance

 ISBN: 9780170448826

4 Look closely at how words are used in the story. On your own or with a friend, reread the story, then do the following.

  a Find as many descriptive words as you can and list them below. Circle or colour those used most often.

  _____

  _____

  _____

  _____

  _____

  _____

  _____

  b Find as many words as you can that are used to show discomfort or pain. Circle the word used most often.

  _____

  _____

  _____

  _____

  _____

  _____

  _____

  c List the things that show this is 'typical' of a horror story.

  _____

  _____

  _____

  _____

  _____

  _____

  d List the things that show it is *not* typical of a horror story.

  _____

  _____

  _____

  _____

  _____

  _____

PART THREE

The writing process – editing

A Return to *your* draft

Do the following tasks. Read the reminders and look closely at the examples to help guide you as you check the accuracy of your written work.

1 Check your use of **capital letters**:
   - all proper nouns (names for people, cities, titles, the personal pronoun 'I' *must* be a capital)
   - the start of a new sentence
   - *no other time* is a capital letter to be used.

Number of errors found ☐ .   I have now corrected these. ☐ ✓

2 Look at whether you have used **apostrophes** correctly:
   - to show that two words have been combined and letter(s) deleted, e.g. don't (do not), I'll (I will), can't (can not)
   - to show ownership: the dog's bowl (the bowl belongs to the dog), Harry's cat (the cat belongs to Harry)
   - *do not use an apostrophe for plurals*, e.g. eggs, blankets, dogs, students, cars
   - *do not use an apostrophe* for words that mean ownership: mine, ours, yours, his, hers, its, theirs.

Number of errors found ☐ .   I have now corrected these. ☐ ✓

3 Look closely at your use of **commas**. Remember, commas
   - are used to separate parts of a sentence from the *main* sentence or to separate items in a list
   - *they are not to be used when a full stop should be used.*

   Examples: Before I went to football training, I had my energy shake.
   My energy shake, which I drink before training, helps me stay healthy.
   I eat eggs, bacon, banana on toast, a cold Milo, and an orange drink for breakfast.

Number of errors found ☐ .   I have now corrected these. ☐ ✓

4   Spelling words commonly confused

Read your work and look for the times you've used the words before.	Get a partner to check your work and put X in the areas when you need to make corrections	✓ when you have checked and corrected your draft
their/there/they're **their** = a *possessive* pronoun. It means something belongs to two or more things, e.g. This is **their** dinner (the dinner belongs to those people). **there** = an *adverb*. It tells us *where* something is, e.g. My bike is over **there**. **they're** = a *contraction* of two words, they + are, e.g. **They're** (they are) going to the movies.		
to/too/two to = a *preposition*. It tells us the position or place of something in relation to something else, e.g. I am going **to** the shops. too = 'also' or 'many' (just as there are '**too** many' 'o's), e.g. I have to work after school **too**. two = a number, e.g. I have **two** dogs.		
a lot This is *always* two words. You would not write 'alittle' or 'aplant'. The word 'lot' is an adjective describing a quality of something, e.g. I have a **lot** of food for lunch. Remember: a = an article (a/the/an), lot = an *adjective*.		
were/where/we're **were** = an *auxiliary verb* (it helps us to know the *tense* of a sentence), e.g. They **were** at home. **where** = an *adverb*. It tells us *the place* something is done, e.g. **Where** did I leave my glasses? And it is also a *conjunction* (a joining word), e.g. I stopped at the café **where** I used to work. **we're** = a *contraction* and means 'we are', e.g. **We're** (we are) students at LHS.		
no/know/now Most people misspell these three words because they sound the same or are written in a similar way. **no** = expresses disagreement, e.g. They said **no** to going out for lunch. **know** = a *verb* and means 'to understand', e.g. I **know** how to fix my motorbike. **now** = an *adverb* and tells us when an action takes place, e.g. I will take his dinner to him **now**.		

Read your work and look for the times you've used the words before.	Get a partner to check your work and put X in the areas when you need to make corrections	✓ when you have checked and corrected your draft
of or **have**? Sometimes we say 'should've' or 'could've' when we speak. The 'v' sounds like 'of' so a lot of people mistakenly put 'of' instead of 'have'. Never put the word 'of' after 'should', 'would', 'might', 'may', 'must', etc. **Correct:** I should have checked the tyres before I rode out. **Wrong:** I could of hurt myself.		
practice or **practise**; **advice** or **advise**? The *noun* uses 'c'. The *verb* uses 's'. A useful way to remember is that the word 'ice' is a *noun*. So, if you mean the name of something, use 'c'. Examples: I am going to hockey **practice**. (Hockey practice is the *name* of the event) I gave good **advice** to my sister. (Advice is the *name* of what I gave to my sister.) If you mean *action*, use 's'. Examples: I have to **practise** my singing. (Practise is an *action* in this sentence.) I have **advised** the teacher of my time away from school. (Advised here is the *action*.)		
brought or **bought**? **brought** is from the word *bring*. The 'r' in the word reminds you that you mean *bring*, e.g. What did you **bring**? I **brought** eggs. **bought** is from the word *buy*, e.g. What did you **buy** from the supermarket? I **bought** eggs.		

 ISBN: 9780170448826

5 Circle the errors in the following and then rewrite it correctly.

My PE teacher which advices me says that eating to much lollies, especially ones brought at the supermarket are the reason I have a sore tummy. Where not going to go they're anymore because I no that I should of listened to her.

_____

_____

_____

_____

_____

_____

B **Putting it all together**

Finally, we invite you to combine everything you have learned and to have another go at writing your own horror story. We have included a sentence starter for you as well as two sentences to use partway through.

Select at least three of the common features of the horror genre. For example: a symbol — crow; powerful verbs; setting — small town.

The house was nothing special ...

_____

_____

_____

_____

_____

_____

_____

_____

_____

_____

_____

_____

_____

_____

_____

_____

_____

_____

The lights flickered and then went off ... _____
_____
_____
_____
_____
_____
_____
_____
_____
_____
_____

A shrill cry echoed in the mist ... _____
_____
_____
_____
_____
_____
_____
_____
_____
_____
_____
_____
_____
_____
_____
_____
_____
_____
_____ ... like they say, there is a first time for everything.

ISBN: 9780170448826

Glossary

abridged   (of a book, film, poem, etc.) shortened, without losing the main sense of it.

adjective   a word that describes the noun. For example: hot, cold, blue, big, small.

adverb   a word that describes the verb (how or when or where the action is done). For example: He smiled **sadly**. They were **nowhere**. **Yesterday**, I went to the park.

alliteration   the repetition of consonant sounds. For example: **T**iny **T**im **t**rod on **D**on's **t**oes. (The 'd' is also alliteration.)

allusion   a reference to another literary or well-known work or person. For example: I was no Shakespeare but I loved writing plays.

anecdote   a story used to illustrate an idea. For example: When I was a small child …

assonance   the deliberate repetition of the same vowel sound followed by a different consonant sound. For example: A st**i**tch **i**n t**i**me saves n**i**ne. The 'i' sound in 'stitch' and 'in' are the same; the 'i' sound in 'time' and 'nine' are the same.

attitude   the opinion, point of view, type of behaviour of a person about a topic, person or thing.

book-ending   phrases and/or ideas placed at the beginning and at the end of a passage.

cliché   an over-used expression. For example: It was a dark and stormy night.

colloquialism   informal language, usually spoken. For example: Howzit going, bro?

compound word   two or more words are joined together to form a new word; sometimes joined with a hyphen (-). For example: babysitter, mother-in-law, homegrown.

conjunction   a word that joins two sentences together. For example: and, but, so, because, therefore.

connotation   something suggested or implied by an object or thing. For example: Black cats always make me nervous.

contrast   the use of words or images that are opposite in likeness. For example: I was feeling hot and cold all night.

convincing   including more than one example to support what you are saying and explain what you mean (magic 'because').

direct address   when the narrator is speaking directly to the reader. For example: I'm interested in *your* thoughts on global warming.

euphemism   a nicer way of saying something that is usually unpleasant or unkind. For example: He was 'let go' (fired). She's under the weather (sick).

extended metaphor   a metaphor is used and then multiple comparisons are added to develop the image.

extract   a passage or part taken from a book or article.

facts/statistics   numbers and specific examples used to support an argument. For example: Around 65% of statistics are made up. She's worked here for 18 years so knows what is going on.

fiction   made-up stories to entertain, persuade and/or teach a moral.

hyperbole   an exaggeration. For example: I'm so tired I could sleep for a month.

imagery   used to communicate visually an idea and/or create a mood.

imperative/command   an order or command for an action. For example: Don't hit your sister.

incomplete sentence   a sentence without a verb and/or a subject. For example: Unfortunately for them. After the rain.

infer   hint, imply, suggest.

jargon   specialised language used by people who work together or share a common interest. For example: Getting **endorsement** for all **subjects** is good, but you still need to have **Level 2 Literacy** for **University Entrance**.

juxtaposition   the deliberate placing of two things side by side for comparison or contrast. For example: We invited both our friends and our enemies.

listing   related words or phrases arranged as a list. For example: I eat toast, cereal and a banana for breakfast.

literal strict meaning, true to fact, not exaggerated.

magic 'because' 'because' is a magic word, as it forces us to explain or justify our statements.

metaphor a comparison between two things where one thing is said to be another. For example: The playground **is a jungle**. All the students **are wild animals**.

narrator the person or character who is telling the version of events/story.

non-fiction a piece of writing based on facts and reality or offering an opinion. For example: biography, autobiography, textbook, letter to the editor, speech.

onomatopoeia the sound of the word imitates or suggests the meaning or noise of the action described. For example: crash, gurgle.

parallel construction/structure repeating the same word class order in close succession, e.g. pronoun + verb + article + adjective + preposition + noun. For example: 'It was the best of times; it was the worst of times' (*A Tale of Two Cities*, Charles Dickens).

perceptive making links between the ideas in the text and your observation of the wider contexts (either the fictional world of the text or the real world).

personal pronoun words that stand in place of proper nouns. For example: he, she, me, you, I, we, us, them, they.

personification when a non-living thing is given living characteristics or when a non-human thing is given human characteristics. For example: The lift groaned on the way down.

phrase a sequence of two or more words working together as a single image or idea. For example: a broken down rust heap.

preposition a word used to show the position of a thing in relation to another thing. For example: on, above, behind, inside, under.

pun an expression that plays on different meanings of the same word or phrase. For example: I've been to the dentist so many times, I know the drill.

quotation direct use of another's words, either spoken or written. For example: As the principal reminds us, 'To lead, you must serve.'

repetition words or statements used more than once for effect. For example: The room was cold. Too cold to think.

rhetorical question a question to which no answer is required. Used for dramatic effect. For example: Who knows?

rhyme the repetition of words with similar sounds. For example: There was an old horse from Cant**ucket**, who ate from a rusted brown b**ucket**.

rhythm the beat or pattern of stresses that occur in poetry and music and often used for effect in prose.

short sentences one- to three-word sentences, often phrases. For example: Try it. Now.

show understanding explain your statements in terms of the meanings and effects created.

sibilance repetition of 's' sounds in two or more words; often used to indicate a sinister event or feeling. For example: The **s**lippery **s**nake **s**lithered acro**ss** the gra**ss**.

simile a phrase that compares two things, using 'like', 'as' or 'than'. For example: They behave **like** monkeys in the classroom, but are **as well behaved as** royalty in the playground.

stanza a grouping of lines in a poem similar to verses in a song.

symbol an image/picture that represents an idea. For example: A dove represents peace.

tone the overall impression of the author's attitude towards a topic, event or character. For example: humorous, sad, happy, peaceful.

use of punctuation the deliberate use of the comma or exclamation mark or ellipsis or other punctuation marks for effect.

use of te reo Māori using Māori words, expression — often without immediate translation. For example: Kia ora, friends, I send my aroha to you.

verb a doing word. For example: I **ate** my lunch, then **walked** to class.

Answers

Part One: All about me (pp. 4–8)

A–E Answers will vary. Check them with your teacher or your parent/guardian. Alternatively this would be a great opportunity for you to share your work with a classmate.

F   Word search

```
R O S R U C E R P L A T R A I T
G L A N D M A R K O Y Z X T J R
E T Q D M Q G N R T L J N N D R
N A Y K W R R A I N X A Q S V M
E P B T L B E C L D R X R W D T
A A I J D T I B R E O M W G Y
L P X N O N V M N D T L H M V P
O A Y A H K L I S S G A T E Z S
G K N T X E T N E I K W G T R X
Y A E B I I R C O A L A B A E P
B H Z R D T N I T I T O E Q E S
Q W N E C A N A T N T B B P L K
M G B V Q R U E E E I E M R Q
L D B O G K E R D R D H B X Y N
T D M R I B A S O I A B T M L S
K Z L P R P J F T Q N Y W X A M
```

Part Two: Words! Words! Words! (pp. 9–12)

A   Match the definitions

a	environment	3	an area or surroundings, especially where people live or work
b	individual	6	**single thing, being, instance or item**
c	evidence	8	something that proves or disproves something
d	landmark	11	a clearly seen object or formation that serves as a guide especially for travellers
e	benefit	2	something that is good or an advantage
f	identified	1	proved or recognised something as being certain
g	involved	4	included; complicated, detailed
h	ambition	9	**a strong desire for success, achievement or distinction**
i	available	7	suitable or ready for use
j	area	5	a region, district; a section, portion, part
k	traits	10	distinguishing characteristics or qualities, especially of one's personal nature

B   Complete the sentence

1	environment	2	individual
3	evidence	4	traits
5	benefit	6	identified
7	involved	8	ambition
9	landmark	10	area available

C   Spelling

1	ethnicity, religion	2	dictionary, definition
3	characters, annoying	4	interpretation, hilarious
5	available, does		

D   Synonyms

Answers will vary, but here are ours.

WORD	SYNONYMS
whakapapa	genealogy, parentage, forebears, bloodline, ancestor
symbolism	metaphor, imagery, representation
ethnicity	origin, identity, nationality, race
inherited	acquired, transmitted, bequeathed
specific	definite, exact, precise
crest	badge, insignia, shield
itinerant	gypsy, nomadic, vagabond, wandering
significant	important, serious, vital
similar	like, kindred
proverb	adage, saying, moral, truism

E   Description of a place

Answers will vary. Check them with your teacher or your parent/guardian.

F   Punctuation practice: capital letters

a   My uncle is called John.
b   He's Dad's little brother.
c   He doesn't like me calling him 'Uncle John'.
d   Instead, I'm to call him 'Better Brother'.
e   Dad says to call him 'Pain in the Butt Brother'.
f   I think I'll stick with Uncle John.
g   I don't want to get between Dad and his brother.

G   Identity crossword

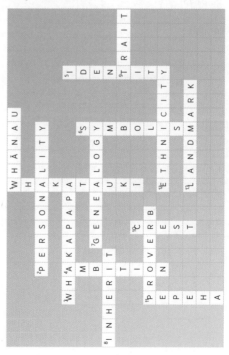

Part Three: Let's read and write (pp. 13–22)

A Match the terms
- a adjective
- b adverb
- c alliteration
- d verb
- e imperative
- f listing
- g short sentence
- h metaphor
- i personal pronoun

B Identity poem

1
- a metaphor
- b adjective
- c adjective
- d adverb
- e alliteration
- f adjective
- g verb
- h imperative
- i short sentence
- j listing

2 and 3
Answers will vary. Check them with your teacher or your parent/guardian.

C Match the terms
- a personification
- b proper nouns
- c pun
- d repetition
- e onomatopoeia
- f rhetorical question
- g rhyme
- h simile
- i hyperbole

D Using texts as inspiration

1
- a use of adjectives
- b hyperbole/exaggeration
- c alliteration
- d listing
- e repetition
- f simile
- g onomatopoeia
- h metaphor
- i personification

2–4
Answers will vary. Check them with your teacher or your parent/guardian.

E Word table

1	E	T	H	N	I	C	I	T	Y
2	G	E	N	E	A	L	O	G	Y
3	P	R	E	C	U	R	S	O	R
4	A	N	C	E	S	T	O	R	S
5	I	T	I	N	E	R	A	N	T
6	F	O	R	E	B	E	A	R	S
7	P	E	D	I	G	R	E	E	S
8	I	N	H	E	R	I	T	E	D
9	P	A	R	E	N	T	A	G	E

Section Two: Our beginnings (pp. 23–39)

Part One: Let's start at the beginning (pp. 23–30)

A First impressions
1 Answers will vary. Check them with your teacher or your parent/guardian.
2 Tūmatauenga, 'let us kill him'; or Tāne-mahuta, 'push him off'
3
- a To tell a story.
- b Answers will vary. Check them with your teacher or your parent/guardian.

B Tone
1 negative
2 negative

long time	wriggling
squirming	swamp
night	black
intensifies	feeding
immense	possessed
never knew	immeasureless
stung	forcing
hide	past
stain	clutch
tense	angry
kill	push
oppressively	

C and D
Answers will vary. Check them with your teacher or your parent/guardian.

E Language features
1

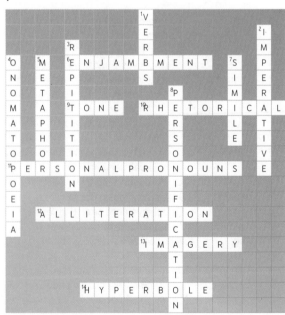

2
- a repetition
- b verbs
- c rhetorical question
- d alliteration
- e personal pronouns
- f imagery
- g imperative

3

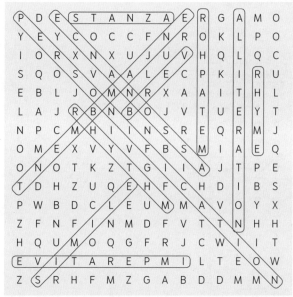

4 a 'We, Who Live in Darkness'; Brothers, let us kill him
      — push him off.
   b This information makes us feel like Tuwhare agrees
      with his narrator. Nobody wants to live in darkness
      and it makes it sound like 'him' is a captor or
      oppressor (rather than a father) and that we should
      rise up against him.
5 Answers will vary. Check them with your teacher or
   your parent/guardian.

Part Two: Making connections (pp. 31–35)

A Kupe and Kuramārōtini

1 a hoa   friend
   b ākuanei   soon
   c Matahourua   Name of Kupe's waka.
   d Hoturapa   The name of Kuramārōtini's
                     husband and the friend Kupe
                     threw overboard.
   e Aotearoa   Land of the Long White
                     Cloud/New Zealand.
   f navigator   A person who conducts
                     explorations by sea
   g inveterate   Firmly established; long-practised.
   h loomed   Came into view.
   i radiant   bright (with hope)

2–4 Answers will vary. Check them with your teacher or
    your parent/guardian.

B Compare and contrast (Suggested answers only)

Kuramārōtini differences: Kuramārōtini named
Aotearoa; comments about being bored being on the
ocean for a long time.

Similarities: Kupe cheated Hoturapa, possibly killed
him by drowning; stole Kuramārōtini; boat was named
Matahourua; tells story of the discovery of Aotearoa.

Kupe and the discovery of Aotearoa differences:
octopus chase; Kupe's wife, Hine, named Aotearoa; Kupe
cut up New Zealand Aotearoa; Kupe returns to Hawaiki.

What did I learn, etc.? — that Kupe treated his friend
poorly; that a poem doesn't have as much space as
a story so the poet needs to decide carefully what
to include; that different versions/interpretations of
myths exist because of oral tradition (things weren't
written down so there isn't just one, correct, version).

Part Three: Push yourself (pp. 36–39)

A Understanding 'Waka 86'

1 Answers will vary. Check them with your teacher or
   your parent/guardian.
2 a Kupe.
   b Those who doubt what he has done/that he
      came/that he has returned.
   c His son; his thoughts.
   d Possible answer: that he did 'more' than
      just discover the land and that people have
      misunderstood about him not returning — he is
      saying that in his mind, he did not leave because
      he left so much of himself here that there is no
      need to question whether he will return.
   e Answers will vary. Check them with your
      teacher or your parent/guardian.
   f Actually, he's only apologising for the 'rudeness'
      of his correcting people's perception of him.

B 1–2 Answers will vary. Check them with your teacher or
   your parent/guardian.

C Test yourself

1 Aotea, Rongorongo
2 a When competitive swimmers Conrad and
      Liam were out swimming one day, Liam told Conrad
      to dive down and free Liam's goggles, which were
      stuck under a rock.
   b When Conrad dived into the sea to get the
      goggles, Liam swam back to shore and left him
      there in the cold water, breaking the rules of
      always swimming in pairs.
   c Conrad got hypothermia and couldn't race
      the next day, and his family were suspicious of
      Liam's part in what happened.
   d In order to avoid trouble from Conrad's family,
      Liam and his own family left Tolaga Bay.
   e Because Conrad said it wasn't really Liam's
      fault, he should return so they could race
      together again.
3 Answers will vary, but here's what we came up with.

TERM	DEFINITION	EXAMPLE
Alliteration	The repetition of consonant sounds	with the **ma**n she'd **ma**rried *Kuramārōtini*
Assonance	The deliberate repetition of the same vowel sounds followed by a different consonant sound	A stitch in t**i**me saves n**i**ne.
Enjambment	Running a sentence beyond the end of a line (often runs across multiple lines) without using any punctuation	I named with parts of me, including my son — I have left my son here, the gods were appeased. *Waka 86*
Imperative	An order or command to action	push him off *We, Who Live in Darkness*
Metaphor	A comparison between two things when one thing is said to be another	the swamp of night *We, Who Live in Darkness*

TERM	DEFINITION	EXAMPLE
Personification	When a non-living or non-human thing is given living or human characteristics	black on black feeding on itself *We, Who Live in Darkness*
Rhyme	The repetition of words with similar sounds	(Answers will vary.)
Rhythm	The beat or pattern of stresses	to my ears. I am sorry for correcting the saying, but I have been returning for a very long time now. (Seven beats per line.) *Waka 86*
Simile	A phrase that compares two things using 'like' or 'as' and sometimes 'than'	(Answers will vary.)
Stanza	A grouping of lines in a poem similar to verses in a song	But then he moved. And darkness came down even more oppressively it seemed and I drew back tense; angry. *We, Who Live in Darkness*
Verb	A doing word	wriggling; squirming *We, Who Live in Darkness*

Section Three: Fairy tales (pp. 40–57)

Part One: What are fairy tales? (pp. 40–41)

A Fairy tales

Answers will vary. Check them with your teacher or your parent/guardian.

B What are fairy tales?

Suggested answer: Fairy tales are stories for children involving fantastic forces and beings (such as fairies, wizards and goblins). https://www.merriam-webster.com/dictionary/fairy-tale

C Categories: Suggested answers only:

Fairy tales: Rapunzel, Sleeping Beauty, Jack and the Beanstalk, Hansel and Gretel

Nursery rhymes: Mary Had a Little Lamb, Humpty Dumpty, Baa Baa Black Sheep

Fables: The Tortoise and the Hare, The Lion and the Mouse, The Boy Who Cried Wolf, The Three Little Pigs

D Word find

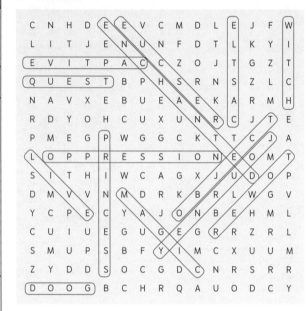

Part Two: Similarities in fairy tales from around the world (pp. 42–46)

A Cinderella

1 Answers will vary. Check them with your teacher or your parent/guardian.

2 **a** Suggested answers: Different cultural influences (what is important, setting, climate, technology, etc.).

  b Because people have always travelled and before the written word, storytelling was valued. Travellers would have shared tales around a fire and cultures could have adapted them to their own culture. Even though we are from different cultures, we value similar things and like to teach our children similar messages.

B Structure of fairy tales

1 **a** Beginning: Pear Blossom's mother dies and her father remarries. The pear trees would not blossom.

  b Middle: Pear Blossom's stepmother and stepsister are jealous and give her difficult tasks to do. Pear Blossom loses her shoe.

  c End: The magistrate finds Pear Blossom's shoe. He marries her and the pear trees blossom.

2 Answers will vary. Check them with your teacher or your parent/guardian.

Part Three: Writing skills (pp. 47–51)

A ~~Speeling Splelling~~ Spelling

1	fable	2	journey
3	oppression	4	magic
5	rescue	6	traditional
7	version	8	perspective
9	familiar	10	prompts

Letters left over: j, r, s, e

B The 'superhero' of the 'parts of speech' family: the verb

a	lost	**b**	enters
c	trapped	**d**	sing
e	turned	**f**	pricking
g	plants		

ISBN: 9780170448826

C Language feature recap

1
  a personification   b alliteration
  c simile   d simile
  e personification   f metaphor

2 Answers will vary, but here's what we came up with:
  a The mountainous giant's voice drowned out all the other voices.
  b The mice's teeth were as sharp as tiny blades.
  c The door to Rapunzel's room was stubborn and would not budge.
  d Snow White's dwarfs danced with delight and delirium at the thought of her return.

3 Answers will vary, but here's what we came up with:
  a The eldest pig's words of owlish wisdom surprised the others.
  b The wolf's breath was a rotten barrel of grain.
  c Sleeping Beauty lay stone-statue still.
  d Prince Charming's heart of a god was what made him brave.

D and **E** Answers will vary. Check them with your teacher or your parent/guardian.

Part Four: Close-up on some tails tales! (pp. 52–57)

A 'The Three Little Pigs'

1–5 Answers will vary. Check them with your teacher or your parent/guardian. Alternatively this would be a great opportunity for you to share your work with a classmate.

B Different perspectives (POVs)

1 and **2** Answers will vary. Check them with your teacher or your parent/guardian.

3 Maze answer is 'Grimm'.

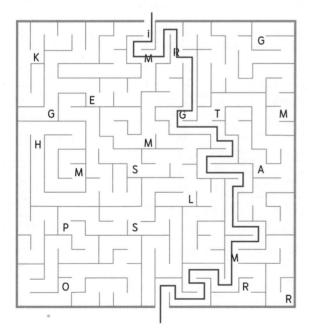

4
  a Cinderella   b Snow White
  c Rapunzel   d Gretel
  e Beast   f Giant
  g Prince   h The Three Little Pigs
  i Big Bad Wolf   j Rumpelstiltskin

Section Four: I have something to say (pp. 58–75)

Part One: Using words to get others to listen (pp. 58–60)

A Identifying techniques used to persuade

Persuade (noun: persuasion)	To induce to believe by appealing to reason or understanding; to convince.
Anecdote	A short account of a particular incident or event, especially of an interesting or amusing nature.
Personal pronouns	Words that stand in place of nouns (names).
Emotive language	Specific words chosen to evoke a certain emotion in the reader/listener.
Repeat (noun: repetition)	To say or utter again.

2
  a personal pronouns
  b repetition
  c emotive language
  d persuade
  e anecdote

3
  a personal pronouns
  b emotive language
  c anecdote
  d repetition
  e persuasive (there are lots of places this is persuasive)

B How to get your opinion across

1
  a A concerned Year 9 student.
  b The Year 12 and Year 13 students make it impossible/difficult for juniors to get food from the tuck shop because they push in.
  c Create a dedicated Year 9 line.

2 Answers will vary. Check them with your teacher or your parent/guardian.

3 Answers will vary. Check them with your teacher or your parent/guardian.

Part Two: Looking at visual language used to communicate (pp. 61–75)

A Image one

1

TECHNIQUE USED	EFFECT	PURPOSE
Colour red	Red is the colour of blood, so makes us think of death.	The colour and font is like in a horror movie when the killer writes a message of warning.
Handwriting font	Personalises it — as if the person is in a hurry because time is running out.	
Emotive language	To connect to our feelings/stir up our feelings.	We are more likely to act or respond if we are affected by something emotionally.

TECHNIQUE USED	EFFECT	PURPOSE
Imperative	Makes us feel compelled to act — we are being told to do something.	Commands are more forceful, usually shorter and people naturally try to be compliant.
Details	Adds weight to the arguments by providing more convincing detail.	To be more persuasive; to answer any questions that might come up that would hinder action.
Slogan	Catchy, so easy for people to remember.	A familiar phrase that is easily identified by others and summarises the key ideas of the message.
Listing	Provides a range of examples to add weight to the argument.	Addresses any questions or gaps as to what might be included or affected by the action/message.
Colloquialism	Informal language that attempts to mimic a conversation between friends.	The viewers/listeners are more likely to take in the message if they feel the speaker is speaking at 'their level' and/or as friends — makes it informal.
Symbolism	Directly relates one idea (often well known) to the idea being communicated so that the listener or viewer can understand the message.	By referencing a well-known idea and connecting that to the message, it is hoped that the listener will have a fuller understanding of the message.
Symbol	Easily identifiable idea.	To communicate an idea quickly and easily using a visual symbol rather than relying on text.
Personal pronoun	Immediately draws the reader/listener into the communication because the message is being spoken directly at the person receiving the message; can also make everyone feel included in the communication.	To bring the audience closer to the creator of the text — to make them feel like they are already on the 'same side' and that it is an issue which 'we' all need to address.

2 For people to stop using terrible, mean words towards others because it is dangerous/hurtful.
3 Plays on the idea of a 'bitter pill to swallow', which is a metaphor for having to take in something unpleasant and harmful like bad words.
4 Don't use these words **ever**; also, stop others from using them/protect our friends if they are bullied.

B **Image two**
1 a emotive language
  b personal pronoun
  c colloquial language
  d pun
  e imperative
  f repetition

Answers to the following questions will vary but here's what we came up with:
2 Stop using straws and chucking cigarettes into waterways.
3 Because we are polluting our oceans and rivers.
4 People don't think of themselves as criminals but, to the sea life, we are committing crimes against them by the way we get rid of waste.
5 a emotive language: killers, suffering, choking, starvation, poisoning, suffocation
  b an imperative: Take Five, Let's use our hands for good and take five
  c use of repetition: take five, crime, killers
  d pun/play on words: the last straw, excess baggage
  e colloquial language: ciggy, take five
  f use of graphics: pictures of common rubbish that affects our water: plastic bottles, caps, straws, plastic bags, cigarette
  g use of colour: blue/green like the ocean
6 Answers will vary. Check them with your teacher or your parent/guardian.

C **Make your own poster**
1–6 Answers will vary. Check them with your teacher or your parent/guardian.

D **Test yourself!**
1

TERM	DEFINITION
Symbol	An image/picture that represents an idea
Imperative	Ordering or commanding an action.
Simile	A phrase that compares two things, using 'like' or 'as' and sometimes 'than'.
Hyperbole	An exaggeration.
Personification	When a non-living or non-human thing is given living or human characteristics.
Jargon	Specialised language used by people who work together or share a common interest.
Cliché	An overused expression.
Pun	An expression that plays on different meanings of the same word or phrase.
Rhyme	The use of words with similar sounds.
Metaphor	A comparison between two things where one thing is said to be another.
Repetition	Words or statements used more than once for effect.
Rhetorical question	A question in which an answer is not expected (asked to involve the audience).
Layout	The arrangement of words and pictures on a page.
Neologism	New or made-up words.

  ISBN: 9780170448826

2

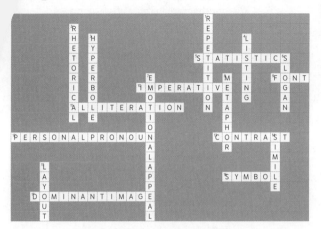

3

1	2	3	4	5	6	7	8	9	10	11	12	13
F	O	N	T	X	R	Y	E	M	V	I	C	L

14	15	16	17	18	19	20	21	22	23	24	25	26
Q	U	A	S	H	B	P	D	K	G	W	J	Z

A	B	C	D	E	F	G	H	I	J	K	L	M
16	19	12	21	8	1	23	18	11	25	22	13	9

N	O	P	Q	R	S	T	U	V	W	X	Y	Z
3	2	20	14	6	17	4	15	10	24	5	7	26

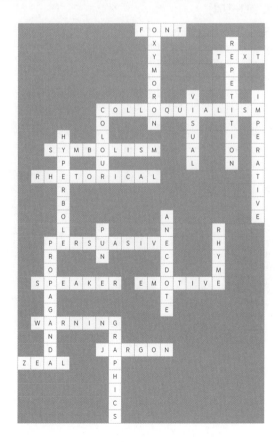

Part One: But first, what is the horror genre? (pp. 72–79)

A What do you know?

1 Answers will vary. Check them with your teacher or your parent/guardian. Alternatively this would be a great opportunity for you to share your work with a classmate.

2
a	dead	b	Johnny
c	boat	d	alive
e	scary	f	here
g	play	h	mother
i	better	j	afraid
k	asleep	l	scream

3 a approach
      withdraw, depart, go, retreat
   b problem
      solution, resolution, answer, advantage
   c abandoned
      adopted, supported, defended, cherished
   d darkness
      light, brightness, daylight, brilliance
   e terrified
      fearless, brave, daring, courageous
   f isolate
      connect, unite, attach, combine
   g dilapidated
      good, undamaged, pristine, healthy
   h rotten
      fresh, sweet, trustworthy, wholesome
   i terror
      calm, cheer, assurance, security
   j cold
      warm, fervid, scorching, boiling

B Setting the scene

2 Answers will vary, but here's what we came up with:
   a Set on a beach, or high in a canyon; 'sand', 'rock'
   b Middle Ages/medieval; 'witch', 'breeks', 'cloak', 'battle'
   c Winter, night-time; cold because fire is lit and wearing of cloak, 'darkness'
   d sights: 'squat', 'pale', 'small', 'bleached', 'black and white', 'albino', 'shorn one', 'sharp light', 'muddy', 'blackened and stubby teeth', 'glistening', 'light'
      sounds: 'bleating', 'cries', 'muffled', 'cackling', 'huffing'
      smells: 'smoking'
      textures: 'sharp', 'sandy', 'smooth and rough', 'coarse'

3 Answers will vary, but here's what we came up with:
   a and b 'All night they had sat' – how long and when they had been sitting; 'her blackened and stubby teeth' – describing the teeth of one of the women

4 Answers will vary, but here's what we came up with:
   a and b 'the offering' – the idea that something is going to be given as perhaps a sacrifice; the potion that kept their minds alert and their bodies awake – whatever they are drinking is probably a powerful drug of some sort that acts to keep you awake

C **Character development**
1   Answers will vary. Check them with your teacher or your parent/guardian.
2   Suggested answers: By creating a calm, gentle atmosphere. She seems genuinely looking forward to seeing her husband, no sense of urgency or worry.
3   Hit him in the head with a frozen leg of lamb.
4   Cooked the leg of lamb.
5   Went straight to the grocery shop and bought some vegetables for dinner. She practised in the mirror first so she would appear normal.
6   Answers will vary. Check them with your teacher or your parent/guardian.
7   Suggested answers: By deliberately building her up to be gentle and helpless (pregnant), so it takes us by surprise when she murders him. The fact she is so emotionless afterwards and quickly works out how to get out of it makes us think she is heartless. Techniques: short sentences; dialogue; strong verbs.

D **How to write a response (long answer)**
1 and **2** Answers will vary. Check them with your teacher or your parent/guardian.

Part Two: Pick a path for your own horror story (pp. 80–89)

A and **B** Answers will vary. Check them with your teacher or your parent/guardian.

C **A horror example**
1   Answers will vary. Check them with your teacher or your parent/guardian.
2   a   To be free from pain/discomfort or to have a peaceful life.
    b   Describing the character in the kitchen making dinner for his boss.
    c   Slicing his finger.
    d   Chopped his finger off.
3   1   q   Making dinner
    2   e   Guests come early
    3   c   Slices finger with knife
    4   o   Lemon juice in the cut

5   j   Blood in the guacamole
6   a   Anti-bacterial cream has expired
7   g   Doesn't sleep
8   h   Kitchen is a mess from the night before
9   b   Burns his finger on the iron
10 d   Blood on his shirt
11 r   Work colleague teases him for his appearance
12 f   Gets more painkillers and fresh anti-bacterial cream
13 m   Fears his wound is infected
14 i   A second night without sleep
15 n   Read about a septicaemia outbreak in a nearby town
16 k   Pain is unbearable
17 l   Fearful the infection is going to travel to his heart and brain
18 p   Returns to the kitchen to remove the cause of his pain

4   Answers will vary, but here's what we came up with for the first part of the story:
    a   stained, neat stack, bloodied, pounding, throbbing, great dollop, the bone biting pain, stinging like white hot fire, tart juice, deep, long, pale, precisely
    b   pounding, throbbing, the bone biting pain, stinging like white hot fire
    c   there is blood; there is suspense; a character does an extreme thing (chopping off his finger); it's set in a normal place
    d   it's just about a finger; there is not a lot of action

Part Three: The writing process – editing (pp. 90–94)

A **Return to your draft**
1–4 Answers will vary. Check them with your teacher or your parent/guardian.
5   My PE teacher, who advises me, says that eating too many lollies, especially ones bought at the supermarket, is the reason I have a sore tummy. We're not going to go there any more because I know that I should have listened to her.
B   Answers will vary. Check them with your teacher or your parent/guardian.

   ISBN: 9780170448826